WELCOME TO MITFORD

Adapted by
ROBERT INMAN

From the Mitford novels by Jan Karon

Dramatic Publishing
Woodstock, Illinois • England • Australia • New Zealand

*** NOTICE ***

The amateur and stock acting rights to this work are controlled exclusively by THE DRAMATIC PUBLISHING COMPANY without whose permission in writing no performance of it may be given. Royalty must be paid every time a play is performed whether or not it is presented for profit and whether or not admission is charged. A play is performed any time it is acted before an audience. Current royalty rates, applications and restrictions may be found at our website: www.dramaticpublishing.com, or we may be contacted by mail at: DRAMATIC PUBLISHING COMPANY, 311 Washington St., Woodstock IL 60098.

COPYRIGHT LAW GIVES THE AUTHOR OR THE AUTHOR'S AGENT THE EXCLUSIVE RIGHT TO MAKE COPIES. This law provides authors with a fair return for their creative efforts. Authors earn their living from the royalties they receive from book sales and from the performance of their work. Conscientious observance of copyright law is not only ethical, it encourages authors to continue their creative work. This work is fully protected by copyright. No alterations, deletions or substitutions may be made in the work without the prior written consent of the publisher. No part of this work may be reproduced or transmitted in any form or by any means, electronic or mechanical, including photocopy, recording, videotape, film, or any information storage and retrieval system, without permission in writing from the publisher. It may not be performed either by professionals or amateurs without payment of royalty. All rights, including, but not limited to, the professional, motion picture, radio, television, videotape, foreign language, tabloid, recitation, lecturing, publication and reading, are reserved.

For performance of any songs, music and recordings mentioned in this play which are in copyright, the permission of the copyright owners must be obtained or other songs and recordings in the public domain substituted.

©MMX by
ROBERT INMAN
Based on the Mitford novels by JAN KARON

Printed in the United States of America
All Rights Reserved
(WELCOME TO MITFORD)

For inquiries concerning all other rights, contact:
Creative Artists Agency, 162 Fifth Ave., #6, New York NY 10010
Phone: (212) 277-9000

ISBN: 978-1-58342-660-9

IMPORTANT BILLING AND CREDIT REQUIREMENTS

All producers of the play *must* give credit to Robert Inman as dramatizer of the play and Jan Karon as author of the books in all programs distributed in connection with performances of the play and in all instances in which the title of the play appears for purposes of advertising, publicizing or otherwise exploiting the play and/or a production. The names of Robert Inman and Jan Karon *must* also appear on a separate line, on which no other name appears, immediately following the title, and *must* appear in size of type not less than fifty percent (50%) the size of the title type. Biographical information on Robert Inman and Jan Karon, if included in the playbook, may be used in all programs. *In all programs this notice must appear:*

"Produced by special arrangement with
THE DRAMATIC PUBLISHING COMPANY of Woodstock, Illinois"

In addition, all producers of the play must include the following acknowledgment on the title page of all programs distributed in connection with performances of the play and on all advertising and promotional materials:

"Originally produced at the Blowing Rock Stage Company,
Kenneth Kay, Producing Artistic Director."

Jan Karon's Journey to Mitford (later *Welcome to Mitford*) received its world premiere at Blowing Rock Stage Company, Blowing Rock, N.C., on September 5, 2007. It was directed by Kenneth Kay,* original music was by William Harbinson, the set design was by Lyle Baskin, the lighting design was by Rebecca Dail, costumes design by Lisa Tireman, sound design was by Gary Smith, properties were by Jesseca Terhaar and the production stage manager was Lisa Lamont.* The cast was as follows:

Father Tim	Stephen Ware*
Cynthia	Angie Radosh*
Esther, Principal, Mayor	Viki Boyle*
Emma, Velma	Kim Cozort*
Stuart, Townsperson	John Felix*
Younger Dooley	Jonathan Faulks
Woman #2, Townsperson	Diane Haas
Russell, Townsperson	Paul Haas*
Puny	Millicent Hunnicutt
Woman #1, Townsperson	Melanie A. Miller
Sadie, Miss Rose	Harriet Oser*
Uncle Billy	Ed Pilkington*
Older Dooley	Brian Seagroves
Headmaster, Townsperson	Steve Sensenig
J.C., Walter	Gary Lee Smith*
Hoppy, Percy	Tom Wahl*
Mule, Larry	Mark Woodard
Teenagers	Cameron Greene, Jordan Rucker, Dylan Russell, Lyle Sterne

Denotes membership in Actors' Equity Association.

WELCOME TO MITFORD

CHARACTERS

FATHER TIM Kavanagh . . . . . . bachelor parish priest in a small mountain town

CYNTHIA Coppersmith . . . . a new next-door neighbor

EMMA Garrett . . . . church secretary

DOOLEY Barlowe . . . . . youngster from a troubled family

OLDER DOOLEY . . . . a college student

RUSSELL Jacks . . . . Dooley's grandfather, church custodian

PUNY Bradshaw . . . . Father Tim's no-nonsense housekeeper

ESTHER Cunningham . . . . Mitford's mayor

STUART Cullen . . . . Father Tim's bishop

WALTER Kavanagh . . . . Father Tim's brother

UNCLE BILLY Watson . . . . town philosopher and joke-teller

MISS ROSE. . . . . Uncle Billy's eccentric wife

SADIE Baxter. . . . . elderly heiress and philanthropist

PERCY Mosley. . . . . . . proprietor of the Main Street Grill

VELMA . . . . Percy's wife

MULE Skinner. . . . . local realtor

J.C. Hogan . . . . newspaper editor

HOPPY Harper . . . . community physician

PRINCIPAL . . . . at Dooley's elementary school

HEADMASTER. . . . . at Dooley's boarding school

LARRY Johnson . . . . adult leader of a camping trip

LILA, LEE, ELVIN, LUKE . . . . teen campers

TOWNSPEOPLE and PARISHONERS . . . . of all ages

handwritten: parishoner — Russell
— Velma
— Percy

ACT ONE

Curtain up.

Music up. An evocation of the village of Mitford—Main Street, the Main Street Grill, church and rectory, Cynthia's house, Fernbank, the hospital. Light up on FATHER TIM as he enters, stops, sniffs the air and smiles.

Music out as FATHER TIM takes a key from his pocket. Suddenly, the sound of a large dog's great, booming voice from offstage.

BARNABAS *(O.S.)*. Woof! Woof, woof, woof! *(FATHER TIM recoils.)* Woof! Woof!

FATHER TIM. Good grief! Get away! Be gone! *(He finally resorts in desperation to scripture.)* Let no corrupt communication proceed out of your mouth but that which is good to the use of edifying... *(The dog's barking fades into a meek whine.)* Good heavens, a dog that responds to scripture. Well, now, I hope you've got that nonsense out of your system.

(The dog starts barking again as EMMA Garrett rushes in, brandishing a pocketbook.)

EMMA. Father Tim! Father Tim! *(She swats in the direction of the dog with her pocketbook and he retreats, yelping.)* And don't come back! *(She hands FATHER TIM a handkerchief, which he uses to wipe his face and glasses.)*

FATHER TIM. Thank you, Emma.

EMMA. That wasn't a dog, that was a Buick! *(She hands FATHER TIM a bundle of envelopes.)* Here's your mail. I'll have your coffee ready in a minute.

FATHER TIM. Blast! Make it a double! *(EMMA exits. FATHER TIM opens one of the letters. He scans it for a moment. To himself.)* Hmmm…from Stuart Cullen… wonder what my old friend and bishop has to say.

(Light down on FATHER TIM, up on STUART Cullen, who holds an identical piece of paper, from which he reads:)

STUART. "Dearest Timothy: You ask if I have ever faced such a thing as you are currently facing. My friend, exhaustion and fatigue are the steady companions of a committed priest and there is no way around it. I'm concerned for what might follow if this goes unattended. Keep a journal. Let off some steam. Spend a bit of money on yourself. Pray. You are vitally important to your flock. Hang in there! I cannot exhort you to marry, Timothy, but I will say…

(Light down on STUART, up on FATHER TIM, who sighs, folds the letter and puts it back in the envelope.)

Act I WELCOME TO MITFORD 9

FATHER TIM *(musing)*. "…exhort you to marry." Well, sometimes it seems sad to have never married and raised a family of my own. But…being a bachelor leaves far more time for my parish family. And goodness knows, I need it.

(A crowd of PARISHONERS rushes in, surrounding FATHER TIM, all talking at once, some of them shoving pieces of paper at him. He looks overwhelmed and bewildered. We hear snatches of dialogue…)

PARISHONERS. …flowers for the sanctuary on Sunday…of course you're baking a ham for the wedding reception…must see you for a counseling session…the order of worship…a new joke for your sermon…Father Tim…Father Tim, Father Tim, Father Tim…

(The PARISHIONERS exit as EMMA rushes in.)

EMMA. Father Tim, that dog is back!
BARNABAS *(O.S.)*. Woof!
FATHER TIM. I know. He seems to have adopted me.
EMMA. Does he have a name?
FATHER TIM. Not that I know of. I suppose I'll give him one. How about…Barnabas.
BARNABAS *(O.S.)*. Woof!
EMMA. Well, keep him out of the church office. It's either him or me.

(EMMA exits as the crowd of PARISHIONERS enters, boiling around FATHER TIM, all talking at once…)

PARISHIONERS. ...Father Tim, Father Tim, Father Tim...

(The PARISHIONERS rush off as Mayor ESTHER Cunningham enters, holding a magazine.)

FATHER TIM. Good morning, Mayor.
ESTHER. Have you seen the article? *(Reading.)* "Mitford is a village delightfully out of step with contemporary America...and while Mitford's charm and beauty attract visitors like bees to honeysuckle, the town makes a conscious effort to discourage tourism."
FATHER TIM. I suppose that's true...
ESTHER. So here we are, trying to discourage tourism, and...

(Light up on MISS ROSE Watson, dressed in a military trench coat decorated with medals, a man's bashed-in felt hat, and rubber boots. Sound of traffic as MISS ROSE directs.)

ESTHER *(cont'd)*. Rose Watson is directing traffic over by the town monument.
FATHER TIM. Well, I don't see...
ESTHER. Tourists! They'll be flocking here from all over to see an old woman in a trench coat directing traffic. I'd like for you to speak to Uncle Billy about it. *(She exits.)*
FATHER TIM. But...why me?

(UNCLE BILLY enters.)

Act I WELCOME TO MITFORD 11

FATHER TIM *(cont'd)*. Uncle Billy. Just the man I wanted to see.

UNCLE BILLY. Well, I'll be et fer a tater if it ain't the preacher. Got a new joke for you.

FATHER TIM *(indicating MISS ROSE)*. Before you get into that...

UNCLE BILLY. This feller, he wanted to learn to skydive, don't you know. And so he takes all kind of training and one day he has to jump out of this airplane. And out he goes like a ton of bricks and commences to pull the cord and they don't nothin' happen, and starts pullin' on his emergency cord, and they still don't nothin' happen. First thing you know, here comes this other feller, a'shootin' up from the ground, and the feller goin' down says, "Hey, buddy, do you know anything about parachutes?" And the one a'comin' up says, "Nope, do you know anything about gas stoves?"

FATHER TIM. That's a good one, Uncle Billy. But what I wanted to talk to you about... *(He indicates MISS ROSE, still directing traffic.)*

UNCLE BILLY. Sometimes she's good as gold, and those are the times I live for. Other times, she's mean as a snake. But it's her illness.

FATHER TIM. Schizophrenia.

UNCLE BILLY. That's right. We been married forty-three years, and I knowed right off she was sick. But she's all I've got, and I'm thankful.

FATHER TIM. Is there anything we can do to help?

UNCLE BILLY. Well sir, I don't know what it would be. The Baptists tried, the Presbyterians tried, the Methodists did their part. But ain't nothin' worked. Now we're coming over here to Lord's Chapel, and we like it, except for all the kneelin' and gettin' up and down.

FATHER TIM. You know, you don't have to kneel. You can stand or sit, just as well. Jesus prayed both ways. We Episcopalians can't heal Miss Rose any more than the Methodists or Baptists, but we'll do all we can.

UNCLE BILLY. I thank you, Preacher. *(Exits.)*

FATHER TIM *(gesturing toward MISS ROSE)*. But what about...

(Light down on MISS ROSE, up on the church office. FATHER TIM crosses to it as PUNY Bradshaw enters, pushing a roaring vacuum cleaner, followed closely by EMMA.)

FATHER TIM *(cont'd)*. Emma, what in the world...

EMMA. I've been telling you you need household help. Well, the vestry has hired Puny Bradshaw.

FATHER TIM. Puny?

PUNY. When I was born I was all sickly and puny-like. I got over it by hard work.

(She exits, pushing the vacuum, followed by EMMA. RUSSELL Jacks enters, carrying a yard rake.)

RUSSELL. Beggin' your pardon, Father, but there's bats in your belfry.

FATHER TIM. Ah, well, Russell...it's been that way since an early age.

RUSSELL. Soon as we get them bats out of there, I'll scrape up the droppings and work 'em in the flowerbeds.

Act I   WELCOME TO MITFORD   13

FATHER TIM. Do you have time for a visit before you tackle the bats?

RUSSELL. I've got my little granboy standing outside. He's been staying with me. His mama's poorly and cain't half watch after him. *(Confidentially.)* She lays drunk.

FATHER TIM. I'm sorry.

RUSSELL. She let all her young'uns go, all five. They were snatched up like a bunch of kittens in a box, one give here, another give yonder. The boy's the oldest, been taking care of them little'uns all his life, nearly. It's an awful bad thing for the boy. I told her I'd look after him awhile. Name's Dooley.

FATHER TIM. Dooley, come on in and let's get a look at you.

(DOOLEY Barlowe enters—a tousle-haired barefoot boy in dirty overalls. He stops just onstage and stands there, fidgeting.)

DOOLEY. Ain't this a church place?
FATHER TIM. It's a church office.
DOOLEY. I cain't come in, then. I ain't washed.
FATHER TIM. You don't have to wash to come in.

(DOOLEY crosses to FATHER TIM and RUSSELL, looking about.)

DOOLEY. You got any place in here where I can take a dump?

(FATHER TIM, taken aback, points offstage. DOOLEY exits hurriedly, followed by RUSSELL.

PUNY enters, pushing the roaring vacuum cleaner. She holds a ragged pair of boxer shorts.)

PUNY. Father, your underwear looks like it's been in a catfight. How in the world do you preach a sermon in these things? *(FATHER TIM is speechless.)* Don't mind me. My granpaw was a preacher and I waited on him hand and foot for years. Next time I'm at Wal-Mart, I'll get you a dozen pairs, 'cause I'm going to use these for cleaning rags.

(As she exits, a crowd enters, chattering excitedly—EMMA, SADIE Baxter, ESTHER and UNCLE BILLY, who carries a large painting wrapped in brown paper.)

UNCLE BILLY. Look here, Preacher. Miss Sadie wants to give this piece of art to the church.
SADIE. I was up in the attic, looking for an old picture of Papa, the one with his handlebar moustache, when I came across this painting of the Blessed Virgin and the baby Jesus that Papa brought back from Europe. Everybody close your eyes. *(They all close their eyes while SADIE rips the paper off.)* Now!
ALL *(open their eyes)*. Whooooo!
FATHER TIM. This is quite beautiful!

(They all examine it closely.)

Act I   WELCOME TO MITFORD   15

SADIE. You know, I've never thought about it before, but this looks mighty like a Vermeer to me.
ALL. Whooooo!
FATHER TIM *(thoughtfully)*. I read somewhere that there's only thirty-five Vermeers in the world.
UNCLE BILLY. Well, I'll be et fer a tater.
FATHER TIM. We'll have to get an appraisal.

(Music up. SADIE, EMMA, ESTHER and UNCLE BILLY rush off with the painting, chattering excitedly.

Light up on the Grill. Newspaper editor J.C. Hogan and MULE Skinner sit at a table. PERCY Moseley hovers over the table with a coffeepot, filling mugs as FATHER TIM approaches and sits. Music out.)

PERCY. Boys, howdy, I got to do something...
FATHER TIM. About what, Percy?
PERCY. Business. It's fell way off.
MULE. Maybe you ought to mess around with the menu, and come up with a special you could run the same day every week.
PERCY. Like what?
MULE. Gizzards. I've told you for years that gizzards is the answer to lining your pockets.
J.C. He's right. You can sell gizzards in this town. This is a gizzard kind of town.

(VELMA Moseley enters, order pad in hand.)

VELMA. I see the Turkey Club has convened. Do you turkeys eat gizzards?

J.C. Not in this lifetime.

MULE. No way.

FATHER TIM. I pass. I ate a gizzard in first grade, and that was enough for me. I'll take two poached eggs and toast.

J.C. Two eggs over light, ham, double order of hash browns.

MULE. Let me think about it.

(VELMA gives MULE a look of disgust and stomps away.)

PERCY. Maybe I could do gizzards with some of Velma's special dipping sauce.

MULE *(skeptical)*. Maybe not.

J.C. You need to advertise.

PERCY. Maybe…a banner to hang over my awning.

FATHER TIM. What do you want the banner to say?

PERCY. Dern if I know. Some catchy phrase, I guess.

MULE. I got one. "This is the best place to eat in town."

J.C. This is the *only* place to eat in town.

MULE. Scratch that.

J.C. All right, let me think about it.

PERCY. I got to jump in here and start cooking. Mule, you're having what the Father is having.

MULE. I usually do.

(PERCY exits.)

J.C. *(to FATHER TIM)*. I guess you're celebrating, huh?

FATHER TIM. What do you mean, celebrating?

J.C. All that money you'll be getting down at the chapel.

Act I WELCOME TO MITFORD 17

FATHER TIM. What money is that?

MULE. Word's out you've got a painting over there worth two hundred thousand dollars.

FATHER TIM. Good grief!

MULE. A Vaneer.

J.C. *(taking pad and pencil from a pocket)*. It's gonna be the lead story in the paper this week. I need a quote.

FATHER TIM. You can quote me as saying it's absolutely untrue. Someone donated a nice painting, but we haven't even had it appraised.

MULE. Oh, and the word's also out that you've got a new neighbor coming in next door.

FATHER TIM. Terrific. What does he do?

MULE. It's a she, and she's an artist and a writer. Blonde, blue eyes, real nice legs.

FATHER TIM. Aha.

(Stage dark. Music up. Light up on FATHER TIM, standing near a hedge, leash in hand. Music under as he calls offstage...)

FATHER TIM *(cont'd)*. Barnabas, time to step outside, buddy.

BARNABAS *(O.S.)*. Woof!

FATHER TIM. All right, without the leash this time, but stay in your own yard. The hedge and no farther.

BARNABAS *(O.S.)*. Woof! Woof! Woof! Woof!

(Sound of VIOLET, a terrified cat.)

VIOLET *(O.S.)*. Woooowwwrrrr!

FATHER TIM. Barnabas! Blast! Leave that cat alone! Come back here this minute! Barnabas!
BARNABAS *(O.S.)*. Woof! Woof!
VIOLET *(O.S.)*. Woooowwwrrrr!

(Music out.)

CYNTHIA *(O.S.)*. What are you doing in my hedge?

(A flashlight shines on FATHER TIM. Lights up. CYNTHIA Coppersmith, dressed in robe and pajamas, hair swathed in pink curlers, enters.)

FATHER TIM. I am trying to retrieve my dog! What else would I be doing?
CYNTHIA. I haven't the faintest idea. Come, then, and get this beast at once.
FATHER TIM. Barnabas! Be filled with the spirit! Speak to one another in psalms, hymns and spiritual songs!
CYNTHIA. What are you doing?
FATHER TIM. He responds to scripture. I'm very sorry, and I apologize. Barnabas, in the house! Now!

(CYNTHIA crosses to FATHER TIM, turning off the flashlight.)

CYNTHIA. Is this going to be the usual behavior of your dog?
FATHER TIM. Quite possibly, if your cat continues to tear through our yard, dispensing with any shred of caution.

① Too many broken items to be realistic

Act I WELCOME TO MITFORD 19

(An uncomfortable silence, then CYNTHIA laughs and offers her hand.)

CYNTHIA. Cynthia Coppersmith. And you must be Father Tim.

FATHER TIM. I am. And I'm sorry we've given you such a poor welcome. I promise I'll make it up to you. *(He holds onto her hand for a moment, then releases it.)*

CYNTHIA. I'm sorry too. Nerves, you know—mine and Violet's. Nothing has gone right with this move. Cats don't like moving, and I saw this man in my hedge, and Violet up a tree, and a dog the size of my refrigerator, and well…

FATHER TIM. I got off lightly, then.

CYNTHIA. Yes! You did! *(They both laugh.)* The movers broke my table legs, dashed a French mirror, dented my grandmother's tea service, and heaven knows what other carnage I'll discover when the dust settles. I do hope you'll stop in when things are calmer. ①

FATHER TIM. And you must stop in as well.

CYNTHIA. Well, good night.

FATHER TIM. Good night. *(CYNTHIA exits, FATHER TIM stands watching.)* A cat! Of all things to have right next door, a blasted cat!

(Light down on the hedge, up on the church office where the painting is mounted on an easel. FATHER TIM crosses to it.)

FATHER TIM *(cont'd)*. As if that weren't quite enough, there's this overwhelming business of Miss Sadie's painting.

(EMMA enters.)

EMMA. Father Tim, that architect called again.

FATHER TIM. I know. He congratulated me on the multimillion-dollar painting and wants to design an addition to the church.

EMMA. And the vestry has scheduled a meeting…

FATHER TIM. I know. To discuss a floor-to-ceiling stained-glass window for the narthex. Good grief!

(The crowd of PARISHIONERS rushes in, surrounding him and all talking at once…)

PARISHIONERS. …Father Tim!…Father Tim!…Father Tim!

(The PARISHIONERS rush off. FATHER TIM sighs and his shoulders slump. EMMA takes a close look at him.)

EMMA. Are you pale today?

FATHER TIM. Pale? Do I look pale?

EMMA. As a ghost. *(FATHER TIM takes a step and wobbles unsteadily. EMMA grabs his arm.)*

FATHER TIM. Something…is not right.

EMMA. Don't move. I'm bringing the car and we're going to the hospital to see Hoppy Harper.

(Stage dark, music up. Light up on HOPPY Harper and FATHER TIM. HOPPY is clad in doctor's white coat, stethoscope around his neck, carrying a clipboard. Music out.)

Act I WELCOME TO MITFORD 21

HOPPY. The party's over, Father.
FATHER TIM. Meaning?
HOPPY. Diabetes. A change of diet. Little Debbie, pies, cakes, candy…outta here. Exercise. Jogging, three times a week. And the most important thing, changing your schedule. You work seven days a week, and you haven't had a vacation in twelve years. Think about it, pal.

(EMMA, ESTHER, SADIE and UNCLE BILLY enter, singing "Happy Birthday." EMMA carries a cake. HOPPY joins in and they surround him, singing.)

FATHER TIM. The big six-oh. How extraordinary. I had forgotten.
SADIE. Father, we just wanted to tell you how much you mean to everyone. I don't see how in the world any of us could get along without you.

(FATHER TIM and HOPPY exchange a look. FATHER TIM sighs, takes the cake from EMMA and hands it to HOPPY.

Stage dark. Music up.

Light up on FATHER TIM, wearing jogging attire. He jogs about, huffing and puffing. TOWNSPEOPLE enter and exit, pointing to FATHER TIM, astonished, and waving to him as he jogs.

Music out as FATHER TIM exits. Light up on the church office and the painting/easel as EMMA enters, holding an envelope, followed by SADIE, ESTHER and UNCLE BILLY, all talking excitedly.)

ESTHER. Well, open it and see what it says.
SADIE. I think we should wait until Father Tim gets here.
UNCLE BILLY. I saw him out hot-footin' it this morning.
EMMA. Doctor's orders.
ESTHER. What he really needs is a vacation.
EMMA. He does, but he's too busy taking care of the rest of us.
UNCLE BILLY. Here he comes.

(FATHER TIM enters. The others are all watching him expectantly. He stops as he sees their look.)

FATHER TIM. What?
EMMA *(holding up the envelope)*. The appraiser's report.
FATHER TIM. Oh, my. *(EMMA hands him the envelope. He stares at it for a moment.)*
EMMA, ESTHER, SADIE, UNCLE BILLY. Well?

(He opens the envelope and pulls out two sheets of paper. He scans the first.)

FATHER TIM. The painting is not by Vermeer.
SADIE. What a relief!
EMMA. Hallelujah!
FATHER TIM. Thanks be to God!
UNCLE BILLY. I'll be et fer a tater.
SADIE. All I wanted was for Papa's painting to hang in the church. I never imagined it would cause such an uproar.

Act I   WELCOME TO MITFORD   23

EMMA. If it isn't Vermeer, who is it.

FATHER TIM *(reading)*. "The artist is unknown, but it was probably done during the time of Vermeer. It has a market value of seven or eight thousand dollars."

ALL. Whoooo!

FATHER TIM. But that's not all. I also have… *(second sheet of paper)* the appraiser's bill. Four thousand, seven hundred and fifty-two dollars and seventy-three cents, including travel expenses.

ALL *(disappointed)*. Ohhhhhh.

(All except FATHER TIM exit. A knock on the office door. FATHER TIM opens it, revealing DOOLEY, dressed in jacket and cap, looking desperate.)

FATHER TIM. Dooley?

DOOLEY *(enters)*. Granpaw's bad off sick. You got t'come.

(Light down on them, up on HOPPY. FATHER TIM and DOOLEY cross to him.)

HOPPY. Pneumonia. We've got our work cut out for us. Russell is in bad shape. If he makes it, the recovery will be long and difficult. He won't be able to take care of the boy.

FATHER TIM *(a long, thoughtful look at DOOLEY)*. Dooley will stay with me.

(Lights down on HOPPY, up on the church office as FATHER TIM and DOOLEY cross to it. DOOLEY pulls off his jacket and cap.)

DOOLEY. Is Granpaw goin' t'die?

FATHER TIM. I don't think so. *(DOOLEY drops the jacket and cap on the floor and starts to walk away.)* Dooley... *(He indicates the jacket and cap. DOOLEY sighs and picks them up.)*

DOOLEY. Stayin' around here ain't goin' t'be no fun.

FATHER TIM *(to himself)*. It's different having a boy in the house. *(To DOOLEY.)* Here, give them to me. I'll hang them up.

(FATHER TIM exits with the jacket and cap as PUNY enters, pushing the roaring vacuum cleaner. She and DOOLEY give each other the once-over. PUNY turns off the vacuum cleaner.)

DOOLEY. Are we kin?

PUNY. What makes you ask?

DOOLEY. Freckles same as mine.

PUNY. We couldn't be kin. You come from down the mountain.

DOOLEY. Blood travels.

PUNY. What's your name?

DOOLEY. Dooley.

PUNY. Don't you have a real name like Howard or Buddy or Jack or something?

DOOLEY. Dooley *is* a real name! You ever try to get rid of them freckles? I hear stump water'll do it.

PUNY. Shoot, I tried everything, but nothin' ever worked.

DOOLEY. I hear if you lay face down in fresh cow dump, that works.

PUNY. Did you try that?

DOOLEY. Nope.

Act I WELCOME TO MITFORD 25

PUNY. How old are you?
DOOLEY. Eleven.
PUNY. I'm glad I ain't eleven. I didn't like being a kid. Somebody was always beatin' on you, pullin' your hair. I wouldn't be your age for all the tea in China.
DOOLEY. When I'm twelve, I'm goin' to whip the horse hockey out of somebody.
PUNY. You better not be using that kind of language in this house. No sir, that won't go around here. You got a mama?
DOOLEY. That ain't none of your stupid business, you old fat witch.
PUNY *(grabs him by the galluses)*. Witch, is it? You know what witches do to back-talkin' young'uns? They boil 'em in a big old pot.

(FATHER TIM enters, carrying clothes and a bar of soap.)

FATHER TIM. While you're at it, give him a good cleaning up. And here are some clothes that should fit.
DOOLEY. Aw, man!
PUNY *(taking the clothes and soap, pointing offstage)*. March!

(PUNY and DOOLEY exit.

A telephone rings. Light up on SADIE, sitting on her porch.)

SADIE. Father Tim, I need to talk to you about something.

FATHER TIM. I'll be right there. *(He crosses to SADIE. They sit for a moment, gazing into the distance.)* Miss Sadie, I always marvel at your view. Look at Mitford...a toy village at your feet, like something you'd find under a Christmas tree...with the mountains beyond. Wouldn't it be marvelous if life could be as perfect as it looks from your porch?

SADIE. I've thought that very thing many times. When Doctor Harper's wife lay dying several years ago, I often looked down at his house and thought, we never, ever know what heartache lies under those rooftops.

FATHER TIM. I heard a Mississippi preacher say that everybody is trying to swallow something that won't go down.

SADIE. Well, he's right about that. *(They sit for a moment in contemplation.)* Father, when I brought you that painting, I started thinking about things I'd never thought of before, about things I've been holding onto—my orchard, my possessions, my memories....and Papa's money. I've earned interest on the capital and invested the interest. But I've decided to start letting go. So what I'm prepared to do is to give Lord's Chapel a special gift, in loving memory of Mama and Papa, and in appreciation for the church I've called home since I was nine years old. *(Beat.)* The gift is in the amount of five million dollars. *(FATHER TIM is dumbfounded.)* This money is to be used for one purpose only. And that is to build a nursing home—with big, sunny rooms, and a greenhouse, and an atrium with real, live birds. It will have books and music and a goldfish pond, and a waterfall running over rocks in the dining room. Above every door will be a Bible verse, and the verse over the front door will be, "Let Thy mercy, O Lord, be upon us, according as we hope in Thee." *(A big grin.)* There, now! Isn't that wonderful?

FATHER TIM *(taking her hand)*. Yes, Miss Sadie, that is indeed wonderful.

SADIE. And I want you in charge of the building project, Father. I want this done right.

FATHER TIM. I'll do my very best.

SADIE. And another thing. That young boy who's staying with you...

FATHER TIM. Dooley Barlowe, Russell's grandson.

SADIE. How is Russell?

FATHER TIM. Over the worst, but it'll be a good while before he's up and around.

SADIE. I want you to send Dooley up here. I've got a list of chores a mile long. We'll see how he takes to honest labor.

(Light down on them, up on Father Tim's office. FATHER TIM crosses to it. PUNY and DOOLEY enter, DOOLEY wearing new jeans and a plaid shirt. He is scrubbed and slicked-down, but none too happy about it. FATHER TIM gives DOOLEY a quick inspection.)

PUNY. ...so I run a tub of hot water and handed him a bar of soap and said git in there and soak. Well, he went to saying how I wasn't his mama and couldn't tell him what to do, so I yanked a knot in his tail.

(DOOLEY, unseen by PUNY, sticks out his tongue at her.)

FATHER TIM. And what did you do to yank this knot exactly?

PUNY. That's for me to know and you to find out.

FATHER TIM *(looks at DOOLEY. He shrugs).* Well, whatever it was, the result seems efficacious. Puny, you're a marvel.

PUNY. What I am is give out, if you don't mind. I declare, taking care of a preacher is the hardest work I ever done.

FATHER TIM. It is?

PUNY. Trust me on this.

(Stage dark, music up. Sounds of hammering, a lawnmower, a weed eater. Light up on DOOLEY as he enters, struggling with an obviously full watering can. FATHER TIM crosses to him. Music out.)

FATHER TIM. How's it going?

DOOLEY. She's about to kill me.

FATHER TIM. What have you done so far?

DOOLEY. This and that.

FATHER TIM. What's this and what's that?

DOOLEY. I took out her ashes from an old stove and put 'em on her 'zaleas. I mowed her yard, took going over twice, it like to killed me, and hit a nest of yellow jackets. Got stung twice. Pruned some old shrubberies, then run up and down them stairs carryin' books to the attic.

FATHER TIM. Aha. What else?

DOOLEY. I eat some chicken pie and drunk some lemonade and eat half a pound cake, and pooped in her toilet. Doorknob come off her toilet door, had to crawl out her window.

Act I   WELCOME TO MITFORD   29

FATHER TIM. Well done! And how much have you made?
DOOLEY. Forty-four dollars.
FATHER TIM. That'll go a good way toward that bicycle you want. Well done, Dooley!

(Light down on DOOLEY, up on Father Tim's office. He crosses to it, sits at the desk and picks up a piece of paper. He reads...)

FATHER TIM *(cont'd)*. "Dear Cousin Walter. I'm feeling better than I have in years. They're not calling me 'that portly priest' anymore. Just this morning, this scripture came to mind... 'Let us, therefore, come boldly unto the throne of grace, that we may obtain mercy, and find grace to help in time of need.' Boldly! That is the great and powerful key. Preach boldly! Love boldly!" *(Stops, ponders.)* Love boldly? Jog boldly! *(Resumes reading.)* "And most crucial of all, do not approach God whining or begging, but boldly—as a child of the King. Yours ever, Timothy."

(Music out. The telephone rings. FATHER TIM picks it up. Light up on a school PRINCIPAL.)

FATHER TIM *(cont'd)*. Father Tim here.
PRINCIPAL. Father Kavanagh, this is the principal at the elementary school.
FATHER TIM. Yes?
PRINCIPAL. I'm calling about Dooley Barlowe. He is on the verge of being expelled.
FATHER TIM. Oh?

PRINCIPAL. An out-and-out dogfight in the cafeteria, with black eyes, a bloody nose, and mashed potatoes thrown in for good measure. And after Dooley threw the mashed potatoes, he followed them with gravy.

FATHER TIM. And what precipitated this brawl?

PRINCIPAL. Ask Dooley. I've sent him home.

(Light down on the PRINCIPAL. DOOLEY enters and looks at FATHER TIM warily.)

FATHER TIM. I've just had a call from your principal.

DOOLEY. That principal preached me a sermon today.

FATHER TIM. Who were you fighting with?

DOOLEY. Buster Austin.

FATHER TIM. And why were you fighting with Buster Austin?

DOOLEY. He called you a nerd.

FATHER TIM. Aha! *(Beat, thinking.)* All right. Go to your room and stay there until I figure out what to do about this.

(DOOLEY exits.

A knock at the door. FATHER TIM rises to answer it. CYNTHIA enters, holding a measuring cup.)

CYNTHIA. I've come borrowing. My nephew is coming, and I thought I'd bake a cake.

FATHER TIM. Come in, come in. Brown sugar or white? White, I suppose, for a cake.

Act I WELCOME TO MITFORD 31

CYNTHIA. White would be lovely. But brown would do just as well. Anything, really. *(Hands him the cup.)* Smells good in here.
FATHER TIM. Barbecued ribs.
CYNTHIA. I just love ribs.
FATHER TIM. Could I serve you some?
CYNTHIA. Lovely. Ummmm. I haven't eaten all day.
FATHER TIM. And how about a poppy seed roll.
CYNTHIA. To sop up the sauce. Perfect. *(Light down on CYNTHIA.)*
FATHER TIM. I'm thinking…she has a good appetite. And…I'm trying not to look at her legs. I need some time to think things through, so I bring her a plate of ribs, then take Barnabas for a brief walk.
BARNABAS *(O.S.)*. Woof!
FATHER TIM. When I return, she's sitting in my chair, poring over a book of lectures by Oswald Chambers, and looking oddly comfortable.

(Light up on CYNTHIA in FATHER TIM's chair, reading from a book.)

CYNTHIA. "Faith by its very nature must be tried." Do you agree?
FATHER TIM. Absolutely.
CYNTHIA. What God does with our faith must be something like a physical workout. He sees to it that our faith gets pushed and pulled, stretched and pounded, taken to its limits so it can expand. If it doesn't get exercised, it becomes like a weak muscle that fails us when we need it.

FATHER TIM. So would you agree that we must be willing to thank God for every trial of our faith, no matter how severe, for the greater strength it produces?

CYNTHIA. I'm perfectly willing to say it, but I'm continually unable to do it.

FATHER TIM. There's the rub.

CYNTHIA *(rising)*. Where does the time go? I must be getting home. This has been so pleasant.

FATHER TIM. For me too. Most pleasant.

CYNTHIA. Let's do it again soon.

FATHER TIM. Very soon.

CYNTHIA. Well, good night.

FATHER TIM. Good night. *(CYNTHIA exits. FATHER TIM glances at his watch.)* Good heavens. Nine thirty! Hardly anyone in Mitford stays up until nine thirty.

(Light up on DOOLEY, seated, thumbing through a book. FATHER TIM crosses to him and sits.)

FATHER TIM *(cont'd)*. Dooley, a couple of weeks ago we spent the day at Meadowgate Farm…Hal Owens' place.

DOOLEY. I might be a veterinarian, just like him.

FATHER TIM. And you rode a horse and it threw you off.

DOOLEY. I'm goin' t'ride the hair off that old horse next time.

FATHER TIM. Let's talk about next time. How would you like to learn how it feels to have a horse of your own?

DOOLEY. Oh, man!

FATHER TIM. Let's say that you and I go out there once a month. And you learn to groom the horse, and feed her, and take care of her tack, the whole works.

DOOLEY. Oh, man!

Act I   WELCOME TO MITFORD   33

FATHER TIM. However, there's only one way we'll be able to do this.

DOOLEY. What's that?

FATHER TIM. You can no longer let Buster Austin or anybody else tempt you to fight. Do you understand? Tell me what I'm saying to you.

DOOLEY. I can have me a horse, kind of, and take care of her and all, but I cain't whip Buster Austin.

FATHER TIM. Nor anybody else. Can you do it?

DOOLEY *(beat, thinking)*. I can do it!

FATHER TIM *(rising)*. And Dooley...I'd like to thank you very much for standing up for me when Buster called me a nerd.

(Light down on DOOLEY, up on the office. He crosses to it. EMMA enters and hands him the mail. He leafs through it.)

EMMA. I've found out all about your neighbor.

FATHER TIM. Really?

EMMA. She paints watercolors for the children's books she writes. That white cat she has? That's the star of her Violet books. *(Beat, no response.)* She used to be married to somebody important.

FATHER TIM. Is that right?

EMMA. A senator!

FATHER TIM. Aha.

EMMA. Her uncle gave her that little house.

FATHER TIM. Um.

EMMA. Never had any kids. (Beat, no response.) Drives a Mazda!

FATHER TIM. With such vast reportorial skills, you might talk to J.C Hogan about working at the *Muse*.

EMMA. That's more than you'd ever find out in a hundred years!
FATHER TIM. You're right, as usual. I think it's especially fascinating to know what kind of car she drives. And how did you learn all this, exactly?
EMMA. I did what anybody would do. I asked her!

(EMMA exits. A knock at the door. FATHER TIM opens it.)

FATHER TIM. Well, hello.

(CYNTHIA enters, holding a sugar bowl and a manila envelope.)

CYNTHIA. I brought your sugar.
FATHER TIM. No need to do that.
CYNTHIA. And something else. *(She hands him the envelope. He opens it and pulls out a drawing.)*
FATHER TIM. Good heavens. A watercolor of Barnabas.
CYNTHIA. Just to show there are no hard feelings—mine or Violet's.
FATHER TIM. Thank you! Come, sit for a moment. *(She sits. He examines the drawing again.)* This is amazing. I hear you write and illustrate books about your cat.
CYNTHIA. *Violet Comes to Stay...Violet Goes to the Country...Violet Has Kittens...*
FATHER TIM. What a full life.
CYNTHIA. The eighth book won the Davant Medal, the most coveted award in children's literature, and the whole thing absolutely took my breath away. Suddenly, all the books started selling like…
FATHER TIM. Pancakes? I mean, hotcakes.

CYNTHIA. Yes. And now I have my own home and a bit of money, too. It's a miracle! But I have to admit I'm weary of Violet books. Maybe next time I'll do something with...oh, maybe with moles.

FATHER TIM *(laughing)*. If it's moles you're after, you can find all you'll ever want in my lawn.

CYNTHIA. You're fun when you laugh.

FATHER TIM. Thank you. I'll have to laugh more often.

CYNTHIA. I was hoping you might be able to come for dinner next week. I think I'll be settled by then.

FATHER TIM. Well...

CYNTHIA *(standing)*. Good! I'll let you know more.

(Light up on SADIE—seated, holding two glasses. FATHER TIM crosses to her and she hands him a glass.)

SADIE. I appreciate your coming.

FATHER TIM. Lemonade and good conversation? What could be better?

SADIE. Father, I'm rather impressed with your young Dooley. He's a hard worker.

FATHER TIM. He's saving for a bicycle.

SADIE *(beat)*. You know, I've gone through all of Papa's money.

FATHER TIM. Five million for the nursing home.

SADIE. So, now we'll start on Mama's money. And I think we should start with Dooley. That boy needs to go away to school...to get the kind of education that will make the most of what the good Lord put in him. Mitford School is a fine school, but at best, it can only try to *make up* for his deprivations. We need something that will *overcome* them! Don't you see?

FATHER TIM. Yes, I do see. And you've put it very well.

SADIE. He'll be in the eighth grade next year, and if we want to get him in the right school, something needs to be done right away.

FATHER TIM. I...don't exactly know how to start.

SADIE. Father, if I'm going to do my part, you must do yours. It's up to you to find out how to start!

(Stage dark. Music up. Lights up on Main Street, TOWNSPEOPLE passing, greeting FATHER TIM and one another. PERCY and VELMA enter, PERCY carrying a rolled-up banner. MULE follows. Music under.)

FATHER TIM. Percy...Velma...what do you have there?

PERCY. Our new advertising campaign!

FATHER TIM. And which catchy phrase did you come up with for your slogan?

PERCY. "Eat Here Once and You'll Be a Regular."

(PERCY and VELMA smile proudly as they unroll the banner and hold it up. It reads: "EAT HERE ONCE AND YOU'LL BE REGULAR." MULE approaches and he and FATHER TIM examine it for a long moment. Several other passersby point to it and laugh.)

MULE. Y'all might want to take a close look and see if there's a letter missing before you put it up out front of the Grill.

(PERCY and VELMA examine the banner wording. They both look stricken.)

PERCY. Oh, Lord help!

FATHER TIM. Percy, you'll be the talk of the town.

VELMA. No we won't! Percy, we gotta hide that thing before anybody else sees it!

(PERCY and VELMA exit hurriedly with the banner.

Light up on DOOLEY as he waves to someone offstage. FATHER TIM watches intently. DOOLEY sits on a bench and opens a comic book. FATHER TIM crosses to DOOLEY and stands looking at him for a moment. Music out.)

DOOLEY *(looking up)*. What are you staring at?

FATHER TIM. You. I'm looking at how you've grown. *(He takes a seat beside DOOLEY.)* Dooley...that girl... young lady...you were waving to...

DOOLEY *(back to the comic book)*. That's Jenny.

FATHER TIM. She's...rather attractive.

DOOLEY. I guess.

FATHER TIM. And you...that is...you like her.

DOOLEY. She's okay.

(FATHER TIM fidgets. He's uncomfortable, in an awkward situation.)

FATHER TIM. Well, Dooley... *(DOOLEY puts down the comic book and gives him a quizzical look.)* I think we, ah, need to talk about Jenny. I mean, it's not about Jenny, exactly. It's more indirectly than directly about Jenny, although we could leave her out of it altogether, actually. *(He stands, then sits again. An awkward silence, then he blurts...)* It's about sex!

DOOLEY. Sex?

FATHER TIM. Sex. Yes. You know…

DOOLEY. What about sex?

FATHER TIM. Well, for openers, what do you *know* about it? If you know anything at all, do you know what you *need* to know? And how do you *know* if you know what you need to know, that is to say, you can never be too *sure* that you know what you need to know…until…

(DOOLEY erupts with laughter. He grabs his sides and throws back his head, then falls to the floor and rolls around in a fetal position, hooting.)

FATHER TIM *(cont'd., to himself)*. He knows everything.

(Light down on DOOLEY, up on another bench. FATHER TIM crosses to it.)

FATHER TIM *(cont'd)*. Wednesday evening. Dinner at my new neighbor's house next door.

(CYNTHIA enters carrying two coffee cups, wearing a look of frustration. She hands a cup to FATHER TIM.)

CYNTHIA. I did it again. I never get it right.

FATHER TIM. Get what right?

CYNTHIA. I sat down at my drawing table for just one minute. One minute! An hour later, I looked up, and the rice had boiled over and the roast had burned, and… well, you saw the result.

FATHER TIM. What were you drawing?

CYNTHIA. Moles.

FATHER TIM. Well, the roast was just the way I like it. Overdone on the outside and rare in the middle.

CYNTHIA. You really are (infernally) kind.

FATHER TIM. Not kind, famished. I jogged today and missed lunch entirely. And you served up a grand feast!

CYNTHIA. You're lovely.

FATHER TIM. So are you. *(They sip their coffee, FATHER TIM stealing glances at CYNTHIA.)* So now I'd like for you to come for dinner at my house tomorrow evening…if you don't have other plans.

CYNTHIA. Why, no. I'd love to come!

FATHER TIM. Cynthia, what *don't* you love?

CYNTHIA. Ummmm. People who are never on time. And, let's see, what else? Garden slugs.

FATHER TIM. Aha!

CYNTHIA. Artificial flowers.

FATHER TIM. Ditto.

CYNTHIA. Loud music, stale crackers, cursing, complaining. Now, you'll be relieved to know that I won't ask you such a silly question. I'd much rather ask you something else.

FATHER TIM. Which is…?

CYNTHIA. What were your parents like?

FATHER TIM. My mother was a beautiful woman with a loving spirit. She could also be obstinate, strict, and cold at times, but usually, only toward my father, who was *always* obstinate, strict and cold. I remember my uncle saying once that my father was a high-falutin', half-frozen Episcopalian, and my mother was a hidebound Bible-totin' Baptist. The North Pole and the South Pole under one roof. Why did they marry? I believe my mother saw in him something tender and felt she could change him.

CYNTHIA. Oh, dear.

FATHER TIM. My father did have a dark spirit, and her brightness seemed to drive him further into darkness. Mother attended Father's church until, as she like to say, she was overcome by frostbite. Finally, he quit the church entirely, and Mother returned to her Baptist roots, with me in tow.

CYNTHIA. What did you think of that?

FATHER TIM. I liked it. Church suppers, hymn sings, a sense of family. It was a simple church, and it caused me to treasure simplicity. It was also where I very likely developed my early desire to be a pastor. I never wanted to rise to bishop. I only wanted to pastor a small congregation, and to weave myself into the life of a parish in an intimate way.

CYNTHIA. I see that you've done that, with wonderful results, to put it plainly.

FATHER TIM *(laughing)*. One of the qualities I like in you is that you put things plainly.

CYNTHIA. What else do you like about me?

FATHER TIME. Now, Cynthia…

CYNTHIA. Oh, just say. And then I'll tell you what I like about you. Complete truth!

FATHER TIME. One of the things I like about you is that you are…fun.

CYNTHIA. Oh, lovely!

FATHER TIM. One of the things I like about you is…your enthusiasm.

CYNTHIA. Really?

FATHER TIM. Yet another thing I like about you is your courage.
CYNTHIA. My courage?
FATHER TIM. It's something I sense about you.
CYNTHIA. Now to you.
FATHER TIM. Do be kind.
CYNTHIA. One of the things I like about you is…you're romantic.
FATHER TIM. I dare say I've never thought of myself as romantic.
CYNTHIA. It's as plain as the nose on your face. Look at the way you love the old writers, especially Wordsworth. And your roses, and the way you set a table with family china, and attend to the needs of your friends.
FATHER TIM. That's romantic?
CYNTHIA. Terribly. I could go on.
FATHER TIM. Please don't. *(Aside.)* Please do.
CYNTHIA. Timothy?
FATHER TIM. Yes?
CYNTHIA. Would you be interested in going steady? *(FATHER TIM is dumbfounded.)* Oh, don't answer now. Just think about it. *(Exits.)*
FATHER TIM. Go steady? At my age? What does it mean, anyway? *(Beat, pondering.)* The truth of the matter is that…I like her. There! That's it! Nothing else is needed. But my everlasting practicality causes me to wonder what I should *do* about liking Cynthia. On the other hand, why can't I simply like her, without feeling compelled to *do* something about it?

(Light down on the bench, up on DOOLEY, sitting at his bench. FATHER TIM crosses to him.)

FATHER TIM *(cont'd)*. Dooley, tell me about your brothers and sisters.

DOOLEY. There's Jessie, she's the baby, and Sammy, he stutters. Then there's old Poobaw...

FATHER TIM. What does Poobaw mean?

DOOLEY. Means he took after a pool ball my mama brought home. Poobaw hauled that old thing around, went to sleepin' with it, an' that's where his name come from. And then there's Kenny. He was my best friend.

FATHER TIM. Do you know where they are?

DOOLEY. Mama said she'd never tell nobody, or the state would come get 'em. I was the last to go.

FATHER TIM. And what about your father?

DOOLEY *(angrily)*. He run out on us. I hate his guts!

FATHER TIM. Have you ever prayed for your brothers and baby sister?

DOOLEY. Nope.

FATHER TIM. Prayer is a way to stay close to them. You can't see them, but you can pray for them, and God will hear that prayer. It's the best thing you can do for them right now.

DOOLEY. How do you do it?

FATHER TIM. You just jump in and do it. Something like this. Our Father...

DOOLEY. Our Father...

FATHER TIM. ...be with my brothers and sister...

DOOLEY. ...my brothers and sister...

FATHER TIM. ...to help them be strong and brave, to love you and love me...

DOOLEY. ...be strong and brave, love you and love me...

FATHER TIM. No matter what the circumstances.

DOOLEY. No matter what the circumstances.

Act I WELCOME TO MITFORD 43

(Light down on DOOLEY, up on the bench where CYNTHIA sits. FATHER TIM crosses to it and sits.)

FATHER TIM. Cynthia…
CYNTHIA. Yes?
FATHER TIM. Cynthia…what does going steady mean, exactly?
CYNTHIA. Exactly what it says. You *go* with someone. Steadily. And you don't go out with anybody else.
FATHER TIM. I already don't go out with anybody else.
CYNTHIA. Yes, but I do. Or did. Or, even might again.
FATHER TIM. What's wrong with things as they are?
CYNTHIA. Things are so…unofficial. I never know when I might see you. It would be lovely to have something to look forward to with you, like going out to a movie or having you in for dinner more often, just simple things.
FATHER TIM. I don't understand why we have to go steady to do those things.
CYNTHIA. Well, of course, we don't have to. It would just be nicer, to know that someone was special, set apart.
FATHER TIM. The truth is, I'm fearful of anything that might interfere with my…
CYNTHIA. With your work.
FATHER TIM. Yes.
CYNTHIA. Typical.
FATHER TIM. What do you mean, typical?
CYNTHIA. Men are always afraid that something or someone might interfere with their work. You could try looking at it as something to enhance your work, as a welcome diversion that may help you along in your work. *(Beat, annoyed.)* I have never in my life argued for any-

thing like this. After all, Timothy, I did *not* ask you to marry me.

(Music up. She stands and starts to turn away. He stands and, impulsively, puts his arms around her and draws her close. They both look somewhat astonished.)

FATHER TIM. Cynthia...
CYNTHIA. Yes?
FATHER TIM. What do you want in a companion?
CYNTHIA. Someone to talk with. My ex-husband was too preoccupied to talk. He was too busy making babies with other women.
FATHER TIM. What do you want to talk about?
CYNTHIA. Everything and nothing. What you did today, what I did today, what we'll do tomorrow. About God and how He's working in our lives. About my work, your work, about life, about love, about what's for dinner and how the roses are doing...

(Music up. He kisses her, then holds her for a long moment in embrace. Music under.)

FATHER TIM. There's something I want to ask you. Would you kindly consider the possibility...that is, the inevitability...of going steady? *(CYNTHIA bursts into tears.)* Cynthia...
CYNTHIA. I always cry when I'm happy.
FATHER TIM *(handing her a handkerchief)*. Will you do it? Starting right now?
CYNTHIA. Yes, I'll do it.

Act I   WELCOME TO MITFORD   45

(He kisses her again. DOOLEY enters, crosses to them, stops for a moment.)

DOOLEY. Mush.

(DOOLEY exits. Light down on CYNTHIA. Music out.)

FATHER TIM. But what to do about all this? I call Cousin Walter in New York, who thinks his own wife is the most compelling woman he's ever known.

(Light up on WALTER.)

WALTER. You love her then?
FATHER TIM. Yes. She's good for me.
WALTER. In what way?
FATHER TIM. Oh, gets me out of myself. Makes me laugh. I trust her. She's real.
WALTER. So, what are you going to *do* about all this?
FATHER TIM. Why should I *do* something about it. Isn't loving her enough?
WALTER. Nope. That's the way it is with feelings like this. You've got to take them somewhere. They can't be allowed to merely dangle around in space. Ask her to marry you.
FATHER TIM. I'm afraid to move forward, but I'm terrified to turn back.
WALTER. There comes a time when there is no turning back. You'll know it when you get there.

(Light down on WALTER, up on FATHER TIM and CYNTHIA.)

FATHER TIM. You are the most beautiful creature I've ever seen in my life.

CYNTHIA *(hand on his cheek)*. I'm not going to ask you to marry me. You'll have to do the thing yourself.

(Light down on FATHER TIM and CYNTHIA, up on SADIE.)

SADIE. Father, I've heard rumors that you might have a special fondness for your neighbor and she for you. Don't be too cautious. I would never tell anyone to throw caution to the winds. But caution can be carried too far.

(Light down on SADIE, up on STUART Cullen.)

STUART. I have the sense that you haven't really given yourself up, Timothy. You're holding onto something, guarding yourself, just in case. Going steady, but no real commitment. Loving, but afraid of the future. My friend, a woman like Cynthia is one in a thousand, one in a million. You'd better hunker down and be willing to give yourself, Timothy, or you could lose her.

(Light down on STUART, up on DOOLEY. FATHER TIM crosses to him.)

DOOLEY. Are you gonna marry her?
FATHER TIM. Well...
DOOLEY. Are you or ain't you? I would, if I was you.
FATHER TIM. You're not me.
DOOLEY. I'm dern glad of that.
FATHER TIM. Why are you glad of that?

Act I WELCOME TO MITFORD 47

DOOLEY. You ain't no fun.
FATHER TIM. Why would you marry Cynthia if you were me?
DOOLEY. Because she's neat. She *is* fun.
FATHER TIM. Aha! *(DOOLEY exits. FATHER TIM stands lost in thought for a moment.)* I've never fully understood much about my feelings for Cynthia, but I understand this: I don't want to keep teetering on the edge, afraid to step forward, terrified to turn back. All I really know is that I feel a great haste to let her know what I can no longer contain!

(Music up. Light up on CYNTHIA. FATHER TIM crosses to her and takes her hand. They stand gazing into each other's eyes.

Light up on SADIE, HOPPY and UNCLE BILLY sitting, all holding church bulletins. Music under.)

SADIE. Well, would you look at this! "I publish the banns of marriage between Cynthia Clary Coppersmith and Father Timothy Andrew Kavanagh…"
HOPPY. "…rector of this church. If any of you know just cause why they may not be joined together in Holy matrimony, you are bidden to declare it."
UNCLE BILLY. I'll be et fer a tater!

(Music up full and out. Curtain down.)

ACT TWO

Light up on FATHER TIM.

FATHER TIM. "Sadie Eleanor Baxter died peacefully in her sleep in the early hours of the morning. I went at once to the hospital room, where I took Miss Sadie's hand and knelt and prayed by her bedside. Then I drove to the church and tolled the death bell…" *(Sound of the tolling bell.)* Acknowledge, we humbly beseech You, a sheep of Your own fold, a lamb of Your own flock. Receive her into the arms of Your mercy, into the blessed rest of everlasting peace, and into the glorious company of the saints.

(Light up on the CONGREGATION, singing. FATHER TIM crosses to them.)

ALL *(singing).*
LOVE DIVINE, ALL LOVES EXCELLING
JOY OF HEAVEN TO EARTH COME DOWN
FIX IN US THY HUMBLE DWELLING
ALL THY FAITHFUL MERCIES CROWN
JESUS, THOU ART ALL COMPASSION
PURE, UNBOUNDED LOVE THOU ART
VISIT US WITH THY SALVATION
ENTER EVERY TREMBLING HEART.

(The CONGREGATION continues to softly hum the tune.)

FATHER TIM. The people have gathered, the trumpets have sounded! Sadie Eleanor Baxter is at home and at peace, and I charge us all to be filled with the joy of this simple, yet wondrous fact. We don't know who among us will be the next to go, whether the oldest or the youngest. We pray that he or she will be <u>gently embraced by death, have a peaceful end,</u> and a glorious resurrection in Christ. But for now, let us go in peace—to love and serve the Lord.

CONGREGATION. Thanks be to God!

(Stage dark, music out. Light up on SADIE, who reads from a letter.)

SADIE. Father, I am leaving Mama's money to Dooley. I believe you are helping him develop the kind of character that will go far in this world. I have put the money where it will grow, and have made provisions to complete his preparatory education. When he is eighteen, the income from the trust will help send him through college. I am depending on you never to mention this to him until he is old enough to bear it with dignity.

(Light down on SADIE, up on FATHER TIM and CYNTHIA. FATHER TIM holds a letter. He looks stunned. CYNTHIA watches.)

CYNTHIA. What is it, dearest.
FATHER TIM. You mustn't speak of this to another soul.

CYNTHIA. I won't. I promise.

FATHER TIM. Dooley Barlowe is going to be a millionaire.

(Light down on FATHER TIM and CYNTHIA, up on the Grill—PERCY, VELMA, J.C. and MULE. FATHER TIM joins them. VELMA has her order pad, PERCY his coffeepot.)

VELMA. Are you going to order, or did you come in here for your health?

J.C. We definitely didn't come in *here* for our health.

VELMA. Order the special.

FATHER TIM. What is it?

VELMA. Ground beef patty with a side of Hi-waiian pineapple.

MULE. How's the pineapple cut up? I like slices, not chunks.

VELMA. It's chunks.

MULE. Give me a bowl of soup and a hot dog all the way.

J.C. Double cheeseburger all the way, plenty of mustard and mayonnaise, and large fries.

FATHER TIM. Beef stew.

VELMA. Cup or bowl?

FATHER TIM. Bowl.

VELMA. Roll or crackers?

FATHER TIM. Crackers. And coffee.

MULE. Change my order and bring me the beef stew. I always like what he orders. But no crackers for me, I'll take the roll. Crackers are for sick people.

VELMA. Lord! *(She rips off the top sheet of the order pad and exits in disgust.)*

Act II   WELCOME TO MITFORD

PERCY. So, how do you like it?

FATHER TIM. My coffee? Black, same as ever.

PERCY. That ain't what I'm talking about.

FATHER TIM. So, what are you talking about?

PERCY. How do you like being married?

FATHER TIM. I like it.

PERCY *(glancing in VELMA's direction)*. If I had it to do over again, I wonder if I'd do it.

FATHER TIM. You know you would. Where else would you get those terrific grandkids?

PERCY. Oh, yeah.

MULE. I'd do it in a heartbeat. Fancy's better looking today than she was when I married her.

J.C. I wouldn't touch it with a ten-foot pole. Once was one time too many. I'd rather be shot by a firing squad. Women want to run your business. They put you on fiber, take you off bacon, put you on margarine, take you off caffeine. Women are always overhaulin'.

PERCY. How about at your house. Are you being overhauled?

FATHER TIM. Actually, we're keeping both houses. It keeps Barnabas and Violet apart.

J.C. How's Dooley these days?

FATHER TIM. Great. Couldn't be better. He'll be home for Thanksgiving.

PERCY. He's not getting the big head in that fancy boarding school, is he?

FATHER TIM. Nope. Dooley Barlowe might get a lot of things, but the big head won't be one of them.

(Light down on the Grill, up on DOOLEY.)

DOOLEY *(reading from a letter).* Hey, I don't like it here. When are you coming back? Bring Barnabas and Cynthia. I could probably use a twenty.

(Light down on DOOLEY, up on a bench where CYNTHIA sits. FATHER TIM joins her and takes her hand.)

FATHER TIM. I love you terribly.
CYNTHIA. I love you terribly also. It's scary. What if it should end?
FATHER TIM. Cynthia, good grief...
CYNTHIA. I know I shouldn't talk of endings when marriage is a blessed beginning.
FATHER TIM. Don't then. *(Beat.)* So, we're in agreement. We sleep at the rectory...
CYNTHIA. ...and I'll continue to work next door.
FATHER TIM. If we ever have a misunderstanding...
CYNTHIA. ...neither will run off to the other house to sulk.
FATHER TIM. I'll make breakfast on Sunday morning.
CYNTHIA. We'll keep our separate checking accounts...
FATHER TIM. ...and never spend more than a certain amount without the other's prior agreement. Fifty dollars?
CYNTHIA. One hundred.
FATHER TIM. Done. *(They laugh and shake hands.)* About that armoire you keep wanting to lug over here from your house for the guest room... Why can't we keep things as they were...in their existing state? It seemed to work.

Act II   WELCOME TO MITFORD   53

CYNTHIA. Yes, well, I like that our houses are separate, but I also want them to be the same—sort of an organic whole.

FATHER TIM. No organic whole will come of dragging that armoire through the hedge.

CYNTHIA. Oh, Timothy! Stop being stuffy! Your place needs fluffing up and mine needs a bit more reserve. One thing at a time. It's all going to work out perfectly.

(Light down on CYNTHIA. FATHER TIM stands and reads from a letter.)

FATHER TIM. "Dear Stuart. Why are women always moving things around? My housemate has moved a ladderback chair from my bedroom into the hall, never once considering that I hung my trousers over it for fourteen years, and put my shoes on the seat so they could be found in an emergency. Tell me, how does one deal with this? *(Beat.)* I hasten to add, I have never been happier in my life.

(Light up on CYNTHIA. FATHER TIM rejoins her on the bench. Their backs are to each other.)

CYNTHIA. Timothy…

FATHER TIM. Hmmmm…

CYNTHIA. Something's on your mind. I just know it. *(They turn to each other.)*

FATHER TIM. It's Dooley. He's different.

CYNTHIA. He hates that school.

FATHER TIM. Maybe we should have waited a year to send him away. He was getting settled here, and all of us realizing it would be a more-or-less permanent thing after his grandfather died, and then I ship him off to Virginia.

CYNTHIA. Have you talked to him?

FATHER TIM. He won't talk. He's hard as stone—face, heart, spirit.

(DOOLEY enters, crosses to them, stands with his back to them. CYNTHIA rises, puts a hand on his shoulder. He shrugs it off.)

CYNTHIA. What is it, Dools?

DOOLEY. Nothin'.

CYNTHIA. Why won't you talk to us, be with your family while you're home for a few days?

DOOLEY. You're not my family. I don't have a family.

(DOOLEY exits. CYNTHIA follows. A phone rings. Light up on Dooley's HEADMASTER.)

FATHER TIM. We've been wondering…is anything going on at school that we should know about? Dooley's not himself, not at all.

HEADMASTER. I'm glad you called. I thought the trip home might do him good, so I didn't say anything.

FATHER TIM. About what?

HEADMASTER. Dooley made friends with one of the boys, and he talked to him about his family, about his mother and what happened to his brothers and sister. I think it was hard for him to do this. I think it plagues him a great deal. The bottom line, Dooley spilled his

Act II   WELCOME TO MITFORD   55

guts to the boy, and the boy betrayed him. He told it around school.

FATHER TIM. Dear God.

HEADMASTER. While we're at it, Dooley was caught smoking on the grounds. He's also skipped chapel a couple of times. I've spent a bit of time with him, Father, he's got strong potential. But there may be equally strong liabilities.

FATHER TIM. What can I do?

HEADMASTER. For one thing, <u>consider increasing his allowance</u>. Even with a few students from lower economic backgrounds, this is a school for the privileged. <u>He sees the boys buy expensive sweatshirts and take off on weekend field trips, and his allowance doesn't stretch that far.</u>

FATHER TIM. Consider it done.

(Light down on the HEADMASTER, up on Father Tim's office where DOOLEY sits in a chair. FATHER TIM joins him and sits at the desk.)

FATHER TIM *(cont'd)*. I'll hand it to you, Dooley, you've never once complained about your allowance, and only once asked for money. *(He takes a check from his pocket and lays it on the table. DOOLEY picks it up, examines it, his eyes go wide.)* One hundred fifty dollars a month. And here are the rules. Get caught smoking again, and you're back to what you've been getting. Got it? *(No answer.)* Got it?

DOOLEY. Yeah.

FATHER TIM. No yeah.

DOOLEY. Yes sir.

FATHER TIM. Another thing. Skip chapel again and you blow off seventy-five bucks a month. Period. *(Beat.)* I talked with your headmaster and I know what happened. Hear me on this. <u>Your friends *will* betray you.</u> Not all your friends, but some of your friends. That's life. Let it teach you this: <u>*You* mustn't betray your friends.</u> Ever.

DOOLEY. I could kick his guts out.

FATHER TIM. You could, but for what? *(DOOLEY looks away.)* Listen, pal, life is tough. School's no picnic. You can make it or break it there. You can stick in there and obey the rules and suck it up and learn something, or you can come crawling home for the world to know you couldn't hack it with the big guys. *(DOOLEY stares at him intently.)* You said the other day you don't have a family. That hurt. It made us feel rotten. The truth is, you do have a family, because <u>we love you and care for you and we're sticking with you, no matter what. That's family</u>.

DOOLEY *(dropping his gaze)*. I didn't mean it.

FATHER TIM *(hand on DOOLEY's shoulder)*. I know you didn't.

(Music up. Light down on DOOLEY, up on CYNTHIA, potting flowers. A clay pot, flowers, a small bag of potting soil, two hand spades. FATHER TIM joins her and she hands him a pot and spade. Music under as they work.)

CYNTHIA. Timothy, dearest, do you like being married?
FATHER TIM. Married to you, or married in general?
CYNTHIA. In general.
FATHER TIM. I do. Marriage is very…consoling.

CYNTHIA. Do you like being married to me?
FATHER TIM *(earnestly)*. Words fail…
CYNTHIA. I want to be your best friend.
FATHER TIM. You are my best friend.
CYNTHIA. <u>You can speak your heart to your best friend.</u>
FATHER TIM. What is it you want me to say?
CYNTHIA. I want us to talk about our future. *(FATHER TIM turns away.)* You're angry.
FATHER TIM. You'll have to do the talking, because I don't know what to say. I don't have a clue.
CYNTHIA. All that really matters about our future is that we're together. I mean that with all my heart. I feel so puzzled about why you shut down like this, why this wave of coldness from you when there's any mention of your retirement? Oh, rats, Timothy, why does it have to be so complicated? All I want to know is…are you going to preach 'til you keel over?
FATHER TIM. I don't know. Why do I have to know?
CYNTHIA. Ummmm. This is going nowhere.
FATHER TIM. So let's get back to work.

(Stage dark. Music out. Light up on Father Tim's office. He crosses to it, sits at the desk and starts reading a book. PUNY enters, pushing her roaring vacuum cleaner. She stops, turns off the vacuum cleaner and stares at him for a moment. He looks up.)

FATHER TIM *(cont'd)*. What?
PUNY. How do you like being married.
FATHER TIM. I like it quite a bit. Do you like being married?

PUNY. Yes I do. Do you and Cynthia ever disagree?

FATHER TIM. Oh, yes.

PUNY. Me and Joe Joe disagree sometimes, too. And I'm goin' to say to you what Joe Joe says to me when I ask him to git up in the middle of the night and bring me a bowl of ice cream with sweet pickles.

FATHER TIM. So what does he say?

PUNY. Git over it! *(She starts the vacuum cleaner and moves away.)*

FATHER TIM. Wait a minute. *(PUNY turns the vacuum cleaner off.)* Ice cream and pickles?

PUNY. Yes, sir.

FATHER TIM. You mean...

PUNY. Twins. And you're goin' to be their granpaw.

(Light down as PUNY exits with the roaring vacuum cleaner. Light up as EMMA enters, carrying a cardboard box. She drops the box on the desk and turns huffily away, arms crossed.)

FATHER TIM. So...the computer's arrived. *(No response.)* Emma...the vestry and the bishop agree, going on computer will bring some consistency to the affairs of Lord's Chapel. You'll think so, too, once we get the hang of it.

EMMA *(turns abruptly to him)*. No way, Jose!

FATHER TIM. No one hates it more than I do, but it's going to happen.

EMMA. I work here fourteen years, day in and day out, and this is the thanks I get? I labor over these books like a slave, watching every penny, checking every total, and how many mistakes have I made?

Act II WELCOME TO MITFORD 59

FATHER TIM. Well, there was that pledge report five years ago.

EMMA. Big deal! As if a measly fourteen thousand dollars was something to get upset about.

FATHER TIM. And the incident with Sam McGee.

EMMA. That skinflint! Anybody can say they put a thousand dollars in the plate and the check was lost by the church secretary! I hope you're not telling me a computer could have found that stupid check he probably never wrote in the first place.

FATHER TIM. Ah, well...

EMMA. So, go and find some young thing with her skirt up to here, and pay her out the kazoo!

FATHER TIM. Emma...why don't you take the day off.

(Light down on EMMA, up on UNCLE BILLY. Traffic sounds. FATHER TIM crosses to him.)

UNCLE BILLY. Preacher, stop a minute and watch the traffic with me.

FATHER TIM. How are you?

UNCLE BILLY. Better off outdoors.

FATHER TIM. Oh?

UNCLE BILLY. Rose is startin' to git so old, she's losin' her hearing. Cain't hardly understand a word I say and won't get hearing aids.

FATHER TIM. I see.

UNCLE BILLY. Like the other day, Rose said to me, "Billy, I ain't got a dadblame thing to do," and I said, "Rose, you ought to go in there and start readin'." Well, she like to had a fit. "I ought to go in there and stop *breathin'?"* she said. I said, "Rose, I didn't say no such thing."

FATHER TIM *(laughing).* Uncle Billy, I'm sorry to laugh…

UNCLE BILLY. Oh, don't think nothing of it, that's the way I do—I keep laughing, don't you know.

FATHER TIM. You're a good one.

UNCLE BILLY. No sir, I ain't. I lose heart, now'n ag'in. *(They watch the traffic for a moment, waving to a passerby.)* Preacher, did you hear that 'un about this census taker going around? He comes to this house and he knocks on the door and a woman comes to the door. He says, "How many young'uns you got and what're their ages?" She says, "Let's see, we got Willy and Billy, they're fourteen. We got Sammy and Pammy, they're twelve. We got Harry and Larry, they're eleven…" Feller says, "Hold on! Do you mean you got twins every time?" She says, "Law no, they was hundreds of times we didn't git nothin'!" *(FATHER TIM laughs heartily. They rise. UNCLE BILLY calls out…)* Rose! I'm a'goin' off with the preacher. I'll be back.

(MISS ROSE appears in a chenille robe, argyle socks and a shower cap.)

MISS ROSE. You're going to see *Jack*?

UNCLE BILLY. Said I'll be back!

MISS ROSE. Be back by four o'clock, and I don't mean maybe! *(Exits.)*

UNCLE BILLY. See what I'm tellin' you? Old age is settin' in to everybody. Rose cain't hear and I cain't half remember. What time did she say she wanted me back?

Act II   WELCOME TO MITFORD   61

(Stage dark. Music up. The sound of birds. Lights up as a crowd of TEENAGERS enters—including LILA, LEE, ELVIN and LUKE—all carrying duffel bags and backpacks, followed by LARRY Johnson, their adult leader. They mill about, chattering among themselves. FATHER TIM and CYNTHIA enter. Music out.)

CYNTHIA. Camping. With the youth group. So this is what a priest's wife does?
FATHER TIM. The kids like you. They say you're a blast to go camping with. Sleeping under the stars, singing around the campfire, roasting marshmallows...
CYNTHIA. Searching for ticks.
LARRY. Okay, listen up. *(Reads names from a clipboard.)* Lila Shuford?
LILA. Here!
LARRY. Lee Lookabill?
LEE. Here!
LARRY. Elvin Miller?
ELVIN. Here!
LARRY. Luke Burnett!
LUKE. Here!
LARRY. Cynthia Kavanagh?
CYNTHIA *(unenthusiastic)*. Here, for goodness sake.
LARRY. Clarence Austin? *(No response.)* Clarence...
LEE. Clarence ain't here.
LARRY. Where is he?
LILA. He and Bo slipped off. We saw 'em. They've been gone a really long time.
LARRY. Okay, we'll spread out and look for 'em. Tim and Cynthia, you go in that direction. If you spot 'em, give a yell or a whistle. Let's get a move on.

(Music up. They all walk about, on and offstage, calling out...)

ALL. Clarence...Bo...Clarence...Bo...

(The stage empties. CYNTHIA and FATHER TIM enter from one direction, LILA and LEE from the other. CYNTHIA carries a flashlight and wears a fanny pack. Music out.)

LEE. Man, you won't believe this.

FATHER TIM. It better be good.

LILA *(pointing)*. There's a big cave over in those trees, behind a big rock. A hole in the side of the hill, kinda covered up with bushes and stuff.

LEE. Huge and scary.

CYNTHIA. Do you suppose Clarence and Bo could have gone in there?

FATHER TIM. Possible. Okay, you kids go back to camp and tell Larry. We'll take a look.

(LEE and LILA exit. Stage dark, music up, spooky. Dim light up on CYNTHIA and FATHER TIM, creeping gingerly along. The flashlight's weak beam falls on a rock ledge. They sit. Music out.)

CYNTHIA. The flashlight's almost gone

FATHER TIM. We missed a turn. Maybe several turns.

CYNTHIA. Why don't I scream for help.

FATHER TIM. Save your breath. We've only been in here ten minutes. We'll find our way out.

CYNTHIA. I forgot, <u>you're one of those men who won't stop at a service station and ask for directions.</u>

(Sound of trickling water.)

FATHER TIM. I hear water. *(Pointing.)* That way.
CYNTHIA. No, that way.
FATHER TIM. I'll check it out. Stay right here.
CYNTHIA *(emphatically, grabbing his arm)*. Don't leave me!
FATHER TIM *(giving her a close look)*. Okay, we'll go together. Grab my belt and hold on.

(Stage dark, music up and under. Dim light up on FATHER TIM and CYNTHIA sitting on a rock ledge, arms around each other. CYNTHIA shakes the flashlight. Nothing. Music out.)

CYNTHIA *(clinging to him)*. I'm terrified. I think I'll scream.
FATHER TIM. Have at it. *(CYNTHIA screams. FATHER TIM says...)* If more screaming is required, you definitely get the job.
CYNTHIA. I hate this. It's horrid. I'm starved, not to mention freezing. Are you freezing? It's…like a grave in here.
FATHER TIM. Kindly rephrase that. Don't you have candy bars in your pack?
CYNTHIA. Two Snickers. *(She takes the candy bars out of her pack and hands him one.)* Go easy with that. Your blood sugar. *(They each eat a bite of the Snickers.)* Should I scream again?

FATHER TIM *(quickly)*. Don't! *(Beat.)* I think we should wait it out. Stop moving and let them find us. *(They sit morosely.)* Cynthia...

CYNTHIA. Yes?

FATHER TIM. I can't retire.

CYNTHIA. Tell me why.

FATHER TIM. I'm trying to get it right, Cynthia. I can't stop now.

CYNTHIA. But you *have* got it right. *(He draws away from her and sits in silence.)* Timothy, listen to me. I lived with Elliott for seventeen years, always trying to get it right. He was never there for me. During those long months when I was recovering from the divorce, God spoke to my heart. He let me know that trying to get it right is a dangerous thing, and He does not like it. <u>Your future belongs to God, not to you.</u> Unlock your gate. This thing about our future must go totally out of our hands. We cannot hold onto it for another moment. *(He pulls her close, she nestles against him.)*

FATHER TIM. Tell me something.

CYNTHIA. What?

FATHER TIM. Why are you especially afraid of being left?

CYNTHIA. Because I was always being left by someone. My mother and father, when I was young...and then Elliott.

FATHER TIM. I'll never leave you.

(Music up. Light dims as he takes her in his arms. She leans against his shoulder and drifts off to sleep.)

Act II WELCOME TO MITFORD 65

FATHER TIM *(cont'd)*. What is this? The feeling of panic leaves me, and in its place is an odd and surprising peace. Somehow, I'm not afraid anymore. Cynthia is right. Whether Tim Kavanagh is in control, whether I get it right, doesn't matter in the least. God is fully in control, and I know it for the first time in my heart, instead of in my head. And knowing that…everything is possible. *(Music out.)*
BARNABAS *(O.S.)*. Woof! Woof!
FATHER TIM. It's Barnabas!

(Lights up, a crowd surrounding them, chattering excitedly--the teen campers, EMMA, PUNY, ESTHER and LARRY. J.C. Hogan snapping photos with his flash camera.)

EMMA. Lord have mercy, are y'all OK?
FATHER TIM. Fine! Wonderful!
PUNY. You had us scared to death.
ESTHER. The whole town!
CYNTHIA. How did you find us?
LARRY. Turned Barnabas loose at the entrance and just followed him.
J.C. What was it like in there?
CYNTHIA. Actually, it was a very interesting experience. So sorry we alarmed everybody.
LARRY. I ought to kick your butts.

(Stage dark, music up, the crowd exits. Light up on FATHER TIM and CYNTHIA on a bench. DOOLEY crosses to them. He's wearing a navy school blazer, white shirt and jeans. Music out.)

DOOLEY. Do I look okay?

CYNTHIA. Dooley, you've become quite handsome. And yes, you look quite okay.

FATHER TIM. What's the occasion?

DOOLEY. It's the youth group party at the church…and… well, there's this girl…

FATHER TIM. Aha!

CYNTHIA. We love you, Dooley.

DOOLEY. Love you back. *(Exits.)*

CYNTHIA. That school's been good for him.

FATHER TIM. Yes, it has. Thanks to Sadie Baxter.

CYNTHIA. When are you going to tell him about the money?

FATHER TIM. As Miss Sadie said, when he's old enough to handle it with dignity.

CYNTHIA. It's going to be a good summer for him, working at the farm with Hal Owen.

FATHER TIM. Hal says he's very good with animals. He'll make a fine veterinarian. But, plenty of time for that…

CYNTHIA. Not as much as we might think. He's growing up.

FATHER TIM. Bit by bit, little by little, he's coming into his own. Something is easier in his spirit. *(Beat.)* I wish I had more time with him. When I retire…

CYNTHIA. When you what?

FATHER TIM. When I…retire.

CYNTHIA. Well…I'll be et for a tater!

(Light down on FATHER TIM and CYNTHIA, up on STUART Cullen, in bishop's robe at a pulpit.)

Act II WELCOME TO MITFORD 67

STUART. Today, I have some good news for this congregation. Timothy Kavanagh, your beloved priest, generous counselor, and trusted friend is getting ready to…go out to Canaan. We're told in Genesis that Abraham took his wife and nephew and went forth into the land of Canaan…a strange and alien land. What did Abraham feel? Fearful of this journey into the unknown, leaving the familiar behind? Of course. But given what God had in store for him, he also felt hope and excitement and expectation and joy! *(Beat.)* Timothy Kavanagh will be retiring from this pulpit and going out into Canaan. Neither he nor I know what God has in store, but He has plans for His servant Timothy, and He will reveal them in good time.

(Light down on STUART, up on FATHER TIM and CYNTHIA at the bench. He holds her close.)

FATHER TIM. There. It's done. Now there's the future to consider.
CYNTHIA. I love talking about the future.
FATHER TIM *(kissing her on the forehead)*. Cynthia, what don't you love?
CYNTHIA. Daytime TV, pickled onions, and cheap ballpoint pens. *(Beat.)* So, what *about* the future? What do we want in the place where we'll retire?
FATHER TIM. Four distinct seasons.
CYNTHIA. With real winters…that freeze our noses.
FATHER TIM. A small house and a big yard.
CYNTHIA. And let's don't live anywhere that's flat.
FATHER TIM. Flat is so…
CYNTHIA. Flat.

FATHER TIM. Right.

CYNTHIA. It occurs to me that we've found a place that meets all our strict requirements. *(They look at each other and laugh.)*

FATHER TIM *(beat)*. Now...the vestry has informed me they want to sell the rectory when I retire.

CYNTHIA. So? *(They ponder for a moment.)*

BOTH. We'll buy it!

CYNTHIA. Were you surprised by the reaction to Stuart's announcement?

FATHER TIM. As a matter of fact, yes. A lot of hugs and kisses, congratulations, well-wishing. Like they were glad to see me go. I thought for a moment...don't they *care*?

CYNTHIA. Don't kid yourself. The backlash is yet to come.

(Light down on FATHER TIM and CYNTHIA, up on Father Tim's office. EMMA sits at the desk with the computer. FATHER TIM crosses to her. She gives him a long, irritated look.)

FATHER TIM. What?

EMMA. If you're going to retire, I might as well retire. And just when I'm getting used to this thing. I wasn't expecting you to give up so soon.

FATHER TIM. Give up?

EMMA. I guess you can't take it anymore—the pressure and all, two services every Sunday, the sick and dying...

FATHER TIM. It has nothing to do with pressure, and certainly not with the sick and dying. I've committed to supply pulpits from here to the Azores.

EMMA. Yes, well, that's vacation stuff. <u>Anybody can go supply somewhere and not get involved.</u>

(FATHER TIM turns away, irritated. Light down on him and EMMA, up on ESTHER. FATHER TIM crosses to her.)

ESTHER. I'm sorry to hear it.
FATHER TIM. Don't be sorry. I'm pretty excited, myself.
ESTHER. That's easy for you to say. When I heard that mess Sunday, I just boiled. Here we've all gotten along just fine all these years, *plus*...you're still plenty young, and no reason in the world to retire. Did Grandma Moses quit when *she* was sixty-five? Certainly not! She hadn't even gotten *started*! And Bishop Cullen yammering about Abraham? He moved to a whole new *country* when he was way up in his *seventies* and didn't even have that *kid* until he was a *hundred*!

(ESTHER stomps away, furious. Light up on CYNTHIA. He crosses to her, downcast.)

CYNTHIA. The backlash.
FATHER TIM. Yes.
CYNTHIA. Dearest Timothy, you are driven to console people, to bind them up, to protect them from the worst. You pay attention to your flock in the small particulars, and most of all, you love them.
FATHER TIM. People are mad because I'm retiring so early. I feel like a heel, like I'm running out on them.
CYNTHIA. Retiring so early? How long have you been a priest?

FATHER TIM. Forty years.

CYNTHIA. What really changed your mind...and why has it taken you so long?

FATHER TIM. My father.

CYNTHIA. Yes?

FATHER TIM. Remember when we were in the cave and I talked about trying to get it right? I figured out that what I was trying to get right was really my father. He was a hard and bitter man who turned his back on God. One reason I went into the priesthood was to minister to him. I wanted his soul to be saved, but that never happened. I believed that if I kept going and never stopped, I could reach people *like* my father, and make up, somehow, for failing to reach *him*. I still feel the urgency to reach people, but I don't feel the bondage anymore. I feel...the liberty.

CYNTHIA. Then feel it, dearest. And keep reminding yourself that you feel it. Give it that...and time.

(Stage dark. Music up.

Lights up on the downtown, people passing to and fro, stopping to talk to one another—FATHER TIM, CYNTHIA, DOOLEY, EMMA, UNCLE BILLY, MISS ROSE, J.C., ESTHER, MULE, other TOWNSPEOPLE. Music under.)

FATHER TIM *(musing)*. It's a good life here. Folks who visit are amazed at the charm and simplicity. Maybe they see the life they once had—something of innocence and dreaming, something of the past they let go, or allowed to be taken from them. They take no time to smell the roses, or count blessings. But they recognize, and so do we, the blessings of living here. If there's no time in Mitford, there will never be time. Blessed be the Lord who daily loadeth us with benefits

(Music out.

The TOWNSPEOPLE exit except for FATHER TIM, J.C., MULE, PERCY and VELMA, who cross to The Grill. The men sit at a table. PERCY holds a stack of menus. VELMA pulls out her order pad.)

FATHER TIM *(cont'd)*. Happy birthday, J.C.

MULE. That's right. Happy birthday.

PERCY *(handing out menus)*. You guys can celebrate by ordering off the new menu.

J.C. What's wrong with the old menu?

PERCY. This is our last year in this hole in the wall, and we wanted to go out with a bang. *(They open menus.)*

J.C. You spelled potato wrong.

VELMA. Where at?

J.C. Right here where it says tuna croissant with potatoe chips. Potatoe with an "e." There's no "e" in potato.

VELMA. You're one to talk. You're the one wrote that Miz Kavanagh is an "a-r-t-h-u-r." In the headline.

MULE. Look here. Taco salad. Can you sell taco salad in this town?

VELMA *(writing)*. Taco salad.

MULE. Wait a minute, I didn't say I *wanted* taco salad, I was just discussing it.

VELMA. Make up your mind. I got a lunch crowd coming in.

MULE. Okay, I'll have a grilled pimento cheese. From the old menu.

PERCY. Do you see anything on this menu saying pimento cheese? On this menu, we don't *have* pimento cheese, we ain't goin' to *git* pimento cheese, and that's the end of it.

FATHER TIM. I'll have the chef's salad.

MULE. All right, that's what I'll have. I always have what he has anyway.

FATHER TIM. J.C., whatever you have, it's on us.

J.C. The tuna melt, the fish burger, and potato skins. That's potato without an "e." *(VELMA gives them a disgusted look and stalks away, followed by PERCY.)* I think we made her mad. *(To FATHER TIM.)* So...what are you doing these days...since you're retired and all?

MULE. Do you lay up in the bed of a morning...or *what*?

FATHER TIM. I'm...ah, writing a book of essays.

MULE. Say that again?

FATHER TIM. Essays!

J.C. I read an essay one time.

(Lights down on the Grill, up on STUART Cullen. FATHER TIM crosses to him.)

FATHER TIM. I keep asking myself...why did I retire? I could have stayed on at Lord's Chapel 'til the cows come home.

STUART. You're not keeping busy enough. Retirement generally gives too much time to think.

FATHER TIM. Don't talk down to me, Stuart. I need a church. My own flock to feed, to herd around. Or better yet, a mission field.

Act II   WELCOME TO MITFORD   73

STUART. Timothy, you're diabetic. You don't need to be stumbling around in some bleak outpost with no medical assistance.

FATHER TIM. I take two insulin shots a day, monitor my sugar closely, eat at regular intervals, exercise twice a week. So it's no big deal. Actually, I'm thinking of something not far from home. Somewhere in Appalachia, where the Dooley Barlowes come from.

STUART. How *is* Dooley?

FATHER TIM. Doing well. Off to college to study veterinary medicine. If you'll recall, Dooley's the son of an abusive father he scarcely knew and an alcoholic mother who gave her children away. I've seen what a difference it can make for kids like Dooley to be given a break, to be loved.

STUART. Well...let's give this some thought, Timothy. And prayer.

(Light down on STUART, up on CYNTHIA at an easel. She wears a paint-stained smock and there are smudges of paint on her face. FATHER TIM crosses to her as she opens an envelope, takes out a letter and reads silently.)

CYNTHIA. Oh, my.

FATHER TIM. What is it?

CYNTHIA *(holding up the letter).* From the awards commission... *(Reading.)* "We are delighted, indeed, to inform you that your most recent Violet book, *Violet Goes to the Beach*, is being awarded the prestigious Davant Medal, which will be presented at a formal dinner on July 14, at the Plaza Hotel in New York.

FATHER TIM. Your second! That's wonderful!

CYNTHIA. Oh, Timothy…

(He embraces her.

The honking of a car horn. A WOMAN'S VOICE from offstage.)

WOMAN #1 *(O.S.)*. There she is! It's her!

(Two WOMEN dressed in garish muumuus rush in. FATHER TIM steps back quickly.)

WOMAN #2. You're Cynthia Coppersmith!
WOMAN #1. We're your biggest fans in the whole world! We drove all the way from Albany, Georgia, just to see where you do your little cat books.
WOMAN #2. We never dreamed we'd actually get to *see* you.
WOMAN #1 *(thrusting a camera into FATHER TIM's hands)*. Would you take a picture of Sue Lynn and me with Cynthia? Sue Lynn, take your sunglasses off, we can't see your face.
CYNTHIA. Oh, mercy. I'm filthy. We really shouldn't be doing this.
FATHER TIM. Ladies, perhaps we could…
WOMAN #1. Just look through that little place in the middle and push down on the button on the right.
WOMAN #2. We just love your little books better than anything. *(To FATHER TIM.)* That little button on the right! There you go!

Act II WELCOME TO MITFORD 75

(FATHER TIM shrugs and snaps the photo. WOMAN #1 snatches the camera from him.)

WOMAN #1. This is so exciting I can hardly stand it. Thank you.
WOMAN #2. Bye, now!

(They dash off in a twitter. FATHER TIM looks a bit lost and bewildered.)

FATHER TIM. Fame...
CYNTHIA. What about it?
FATHER TIM. ...can never be a bedfellow to tranquility.
CYNTHIA. And all because of little books about a cat. Who knew? *(Light down on her.)*
FATHER TIM. What is this? Am I jealous of my wife's fame? I pray for humility, for help in swallowing my pride. But is it pride, or a deeper issue? Fear. I'm afraid she'd somehow be taken from me, swept away on a tide we can't anticipate or control. [Aside]

(Light up on HOPPY, holding a clipboard. FATHER TIM crosses to him.)

HOPPY. Your glucometer reading is through the roof. What happened to your exercise program?
FATHER TIM. Let's see...
HOPPY. You've got to get back on a strict exercise regime and watch your diet. Plus, I'm going to double your insulin...ten more units every day. Every morning, every evening, no cutbacks, no slip-ups, and no excuses. *(FATHER TIM nods despondently.)* I'm worried about

you, pal. I don't think you've ever realized how serious this can be.

FATHER TIM. Maybe not. I've tried to stay with the exercise, but lately I haven't felt up to it.

HOPPY. That's when you need to push yourself to do it, of course.

FATHER TIM. Of course.

(Stage dark.)

FATHER TIM *(V.O., cont'd)*. Okay, I did for a while. But then I get ravenously hungry and cut back on my insulin, and find myself in a kind of funk, a gray fog, feeling disoriented...

(Music up, foreboding and ominous. The roar of a car's engine, squealing tires, a crash of splintering glass and tortured metal. Flashing blue and red lights.

Light up on FATHER TIM in a wheelchair, CYNTHIA at his side. Music out.

HOPPY enters. He looks weary and frustrated.)

HOPPY. Dear God, what bloody foolishness! How many times are you going to pull this stunt? What the devil did you do to yourself, anyway?

FATHER TIM. I don't remember. What happened?

HOPPY *(angrily)*. You blacked out while you were driving. Hit a stop sign. Weren't wearing your seat belt. Whacked your head and got a concussion. You were co-

Act II   WELCOME TO MITFORD   77

matose for forty-eight hours. You've cut back on your insulin, haven't you.
FATHER TIM. A little.
HOPPY. What did you eat…cake?
FATHER TIM. Not cake, Coke. I had a Coke at a country store on the way home.
HOPPY *(shaking his head).* I don't know. I just don't know. You're a pain in the butt.

(Stage dark. Voices…)

— tape recording

ESTHER *(V.O.).* Everybody in town's calling, wanting to know how he's doing.
CYNTHIA *(V.O.).* Going home today, but he's looking at a full month of recovery. Hoppy says he'll feel rotten for six weeks.

(Sound of a vacuum cleaner.)

PUNY *(V.O.).* Gettin' everything in good shape. Lordy, it'll be good to have him back.

(Light up on two wingback chairs. From offstage…)

CYNTHIA *(O.S.).* Barnabas, look who's here.
BARNABAS. Woof! Woof!

(FATHER TIM enters, shuffling slowly along in slippers. He settles into one of the chairs.)

FATHER TIM. I have come home. *(But there is no joy in it. He looks around mournfully, sighs, leans back in the chair and closes his eyes. Voices…)*
EMMA *(O.S.)*. But I've brought his emails.
CYNTHIA *(O.S.)*. No more emails. He needs rest.
EMMA *(O.S., crankily)*. You'd think some company would do him good.
CYNTHIA *(O.S.)*. No more *anything* for a while.

(Sound of the rather forceful closing of a door. CYNTHIA enters, crosses to him, and sits in the other chair.)

CYNTHIA *(cont'd)*. Emma.
FATHER TIM. I would like to have seen her.
CYNTHIA. No visitors. Doctor's orders.
FATHER TIM. Where's Puny?
CYNTHIA. I've given her a few days off. *(They stare at each other for a moment.)* There's something you need to know, and I believe you're strong enough to hear it. When you blacked out, you did hit the stop sign, but you also hit Bill Sprouse, the Baptist minister. And his dog Sparky. Bill is in the hospital with several fractures and a mild concussion. Sparky was found under the rear wheel of your car. We think he died instantly.
FATHER TIM. Lord have mercy.
CYNTHIA. The good news is that Bill will be all right, though he'll need several weeks to heal.

(FATHER TIM looks bleakly at her. Light down. CYNTHIA exits. Light up. OLDER DOOLEY enters, crosses to him and sits.)

DOOLEY. I'm sorry.
FATHER TIM. I know.
DOOLEY. I would do something if I could.
FATHER TIM. I know.
DOOLEY. I've been praying for you.
FATHER TIM. Don't stop.
DOOLEY. No sir, I won't. *(They sit for a moment in silence. DOOLEY rises and hugs him.)* I'd better go.
FATHER TIM. I know.
DOOLEY *(voice shaking)*. I love you.

(FATHER TIM can only nod. DOOLEY exits. HOPPY enters and sits.)

HOPPY. Depression. And don't think it's unusual after what you've been through. Depression usually stems from anger turned inward. I suggest you look at what the anger is about. Get to the root of it. I'm going to change your medication, but more important, I want you to start seeing people.
FATHER TIM. I don't want to see anyone.
HOPPY. Doctor's orders.
FATHER TIM. It was doctor's orders that I *not* have company.
HOPPY. That was then. This is now.

(Light down. HOPPY exits. CYNTHIA enters and crosses to FATHER TIM as light comes up. She bends and kisses his forehead.)

CYNTHIA. Happy birthday, sweetheart.

FATHER TIM. I'm sorry I can't be more...I can't be everything you need.
CYNTHIA. But you are everything I need. This will pass away, Timothy, this difficult time is not for all eternity. Remember Jeremiah: "I know the plans I have for you, says the Lord, plans for good and not for evil, to give you a future and a hope." I am praying that God will use this hard thing for good. *(Beat.)* And now...I've invited a few friends to visit on your birthday. One at a time. You're going to have fun today.
FATHER TIM. Do I have to?

(CYNTHIA gives him a wry look, kisses him again and exits. UNCLE BILLY enters and crosses to him.)

UNCLE BILLY. Rose couldn't come, she was peelin' taters for supper.
FATHER TIM. Aha.
UNCLE BILLY. I've come to tell a joke for your birthday.
FATHER TIM. Is that right? Well, I appreciate it.
UNCLE BILLY. All right, here goes. Three preachers was settin' around talkin', don't you know. First 'un said, "You'uns ought to see the bats I've got a'flyin' around in my church attic. I've tried about everything, but nothin' scares 'em off." Next 'un said, "Law, we've got hundreds of 'em livin' in our belfry. I've done had the whole place fumigated, but cain't git rid of 'em at all." Last 'un said, "Shoot, I baptized every one of mine, made 'em members of the church, an' ain't seen nary one since." *(FATHER TIM stares for a moment, then makes a feeble attempt to laugh.)* Didn't go over too good, did it?

Act II   WELCOME TO MITFORD   81

FATHER TIM. I'm sorry, Uncle Billy, it's a good joke, really it is. I'm just not...

UNCLE BILLY. I ain't goin' to take it personal, Preacher. No sir! We're goin' to try again is what we're goin' to do. *(He rises.)* You'uns just set right there a day or two and I'll be back, don't you know. *(Calling offstage.)* I'm through with my turn, Miz Kavanagh.

CYNTHIA *(O.S.)*. There's cake and ice cream in the kitchen.

(UNCLE BILLY exits. EMMA enters, carrying a sheet of paper.)

EMMA. I can't believe I'm seeing you. I was beginning to wonder if you were dead or alive.

FATHER TIM. All of the above.

EMMA *(takes a seat)*. Well, happy birthday. I've been on the Internet.

FATHER TIM. And?

EMMA. I found some good stuff. Listen to this one. *(Reads.)* "Read the Bible, it'll scare the hell out of you." *(Dull silence.)* You're not laughing.

FATHER TIM. It's not funny.

EMMA. I laughed. *(No response.)* All right, here's some blooper headlines I found. The kind J.C. Hogan writes, only better. *(Reading.)* "War Dims Hope for Peace." *(No response.)* That's *funny*. *(No response.)* All right, here's some more. "Typhoon Rips Through Cemetery; Hundreds Dead." "Don't let worry kill you, let the church help." "Stolen Painting Found by Tree."

FATHER TIM. I don't get it.

EMMA. You wouldn't.

(EMMA rises and exits. STUART Cullen enters and sits.)

STUART. Do you feel like telling me everything?

FATHER TIM. I blacked out at the wheel of my car and hit Bill Sprouse...

STUART. I know all that, and God knows, I'm sorry. What I'd really like to hear is how you are in your soul.

FATHER TIM. Ah, my soul.

STUART. Let's pray. *(He takes FATHER TIM's hand, they bow heads.)* Heavenly Father, giver of life and health, comfort and hope, please visit us with a strong sense of Your presence, that we may trust in Your strength, Your wisdom, and Your love. We ask Your grace especially upon Timothy, that he may know Your gift of a heart made joyous and strong by faith. Bless Cynthia, too, whose eager hands and heart care for him. *(Heads bowed for a moment longer, then STUART rises.)* He will put things right, Timothy, and don't forget it.

FATHER TIM. The Lord be with you, Stuart.

STUART. And also with you.

(STUART exits. PUNY enters, pushing the roaring vacuum cleaner. She crosses to FATHER TIM, gives him a once-over, and turns it off.)

FATHER TIM. Puny! I've missed you! *pats chair* How are the girls?

PUNY. Just fine. I'll bring 'em to see you Sunday. ~~*(She starts the vacuum cleaner again.)*~~

FATHER TIM. Puny... ~~*(She turns it off.)*~~ What are they saying on the street?

PUNY. They're saying it could've been a whole lot worse. Nobody holds it against you. *(sits)*

Props are not attached to the ground. The actor should move them when needed.

Act II WELCOME TO MITFORD 83

FATHER TIM. Nobody?

PUNY. No sir. And if you don't mind me saying, I wish you wouldn't hold it against yourself. *(Beat.)* I couldn't stand it if anything happened to you.

FATHER TIM. Puny, I feel the very same way about you.

PUNY. You ain't been yourself.

FATHER TIM. Who have I been, do you think?

PUNY. Somebody sad ... and grouchy.

FATHER TIM. Aha.

PUNY. Are you going to git back to your old self?

FATHER TIM. I'll try, Puny. I'm going to try.

PUNY. Good. I hope you make it snappy.

(She starts the vacuum cleaner again and exits with it.

Light down on the chairs, up on J.C. Hogan, who reads from a newspaper.)

J.C. "Mitford's biggest celebrity, Ms. Cynthia Coppersmith Kavanagh, will travel to New York City on Thursday to receive one of publishing's highest honors. In a ceremony at the Waldorf Astoria, she will be given her second Davant Medal in recognition of her series of books about a white cat, Violet, who is an actual cat that lives right here in Mitford with Ms. Kavanagh and her husband. No other *arthur* has won the medal twice. Insiders say the Davant Medal is right up there with an Oscar. Ms. Kavanagh will be accompanied to New York by Dooley Russell Barlowe of Mitford, who is a rising college sophomore."

(Light down on J.C., up on FATHER TIM and DOOLEY.)

FATHER TIM. Give her your arm when you cross the street. Like this. *(He demonstrates.)*

DOOLEY. Why?

FATHER TIM. Because there's a lot of traffic in New York and it's dangerous up there. Because she's a woman. And because as a man, it's your job.

DOOLEY. I'll take care of her, I promise.

FATHER TIM. She's got our credit card, but you make the arrangements. Pick a good restaurant. She likes French or Italian. Call ahead for a reservation.

DOOLEY. OK. Cool.

FATHER TIM *(fishing in his pocket)*. Here's a hundred bucks. Hold onto your wallet. Help Cynthia watch her pocketbook. Do you need to write any of this down?

DOOLEY. No sir.

FATHER TIM. Good. On second thought *(back to his pocket)* here's another hundred, just in case. And twenty for you.

DOOLEY. Wow. I always wanted to carry this stuff around.

FATHER TIM. One more thing. If you pass a flower stall, buy flowers. Pink roses, no red…or tulips if they don't have roses. A dozen. Tell her they're from me.

DOOLEY. Yes sir.

FATHER TIM. Any questions?

DOOLEY. No sir.

FATHER TIM. Well done!

DOOLEY *(starts to exit, then turns back)*. I *do* have a question. Or…I want to ask you to do something.

FATHER TIM. Yes?

DOOLEY. I want you and Cynthia to adopt me. I want to take your name.

FATHER TIM. You're sure, Dooley.
DOOLEY. Yes sir.

(They embrace. Music up.)

Light down on DOOLEY. He exits. Music out.)

FATHER TIM. I'm looking for something in the Scriptures these days…a specific message from God. I don't know what it might be, but I know it will be direct, meant profoundly for me, and that I'll recognize it the instant it's revealed.

(Music out, lights up on the Grill where PERCY is wiping off a table. FATHER TIM approaches.)

PERCY. I ain't believing my eyes. I thought you'd dropped off the face of the earth. It's been a month, at least.
FATHER TIM. Back again and feeling better. It's great to see you, Buddyroe. *(FATHER TIM takes a seat.)*
PERCY. I ain't poached an egg since the last time you was in here.
FATHER TIM. We'll see if you've lost your touch. I'll have two poached on whole wheat, the usual. And cantaloupe. I've been craving a good cantaloupe.
PERCY *(writes the order on a pad)*. The Turkey Club ain't been the same with you gone.

(J.C. enters, carrying a newspaper, and takes a chair.)

J.C. Hot off the press, all the news that's fit to print, you heard it here first. *(FATHER TIM reaches for the paper.)* That'll be fifty cents.

FATHER TIM. Fifty cents?

(MULE enters and crosses to the table.)

J.C. Paper's gone up, ink's gone up, distribution's gone up...

MULE *(taking a seat)*. Quality's gone down.

PERCY. Ten cents worth of news for half a dollar.

J.C. *(to PERCY)*. While you're preaching, let me have a quarter's worth of sausage biscuit for a dollar, with a twenty-cent side of hash browns for a dollar seventy-five.

PERCY. Turkey. *(To MULE.)* You?

MULE. I'll have to think about it.

PERCY. Turkey. *(He exits, jotting on the order pad.)*

J.C. So...look at the front page. *(He hands the paper to FATHER TIM, who holds it up, revealing a photo of CYNTHIA receiving the medal.)*

FATHER TIM *(reading headline)*. "Prestigious Davant Metal Bestowed on Local Author."

J.C. I guess "bestowed" is kind of a big word for a small-town paper, but I figured that learning a new word could be educational.

FATHER TIM. Aha.

MULE. So, how was her trip to New York...she and Dooley?

FATHER TIM. Excellent. Dooley enjoyed it as much as she did. She bought him an Italian suit. And a silk tie.

J.C., MULE. Good Lord!

FATHER TIM. Yes, that's what I said.

Act II   WELCOME TO MITFORD   87

MULE. So, Buddyroe, welcome back.
FATHER TIM. Thanks. Glad to be back. Looks like nothing's changed.
MULE. Same ol', same ol'.

(Light down on the Grill, up on a bench where CYNTHIA sits. He joins her and takes her hand.)

CYNTHIA. I missed my husband.
FATHER TIM. I missed my wife…my extravagant, generous, witty, and important wife.
CYNTHIA. I love it when you talk like that.
FATHER TIM. Ah, Kavanagh, what don't you love?
CYNTHIA. Taxis that go ninety miles an hour in midtown traffic, pantyhose that are a size too small, which one can't *know* until dressing for the awards dinner, then it's too late, and, of course, age spots.
FATHER TIM *(laughing)*. That about covers it. *(He puts his arm around her. They sit for a moment, gazing into each other's eyes.)* I was afraid…of losing you to your success. I wondered if it would overshadow what we had.
CYNTHIA. Nothing can do that, Timothy. And you can never, ever lose me. I refuse to be lost. (Funny line)
FATHER TIM. I love you, Kavanagh. Madly.
CYNTHIA. I love you madly back. And so do a lot of other people. Father Talbot called just now. He's hoping you can supply at Lord's Chapel when he's on vacation. He said it would make a lot of people happy.
FATHER TIM *(pondering it intently, then…)*. Yes. I'd like nothing better.

(Stage dark. Music up, then under.

Dim light up on FATHER TIM, asleep in a wingback chair, a Bible in his lap. A clock chimes two. He wakes, then opens the Bible and begins to leaf through it.)

FATHER TIM *(cont'd)*. Lord, speak to me, please, in a way I can understand clearly. I've read Your word, I've sought Your counsel, and I've waited. You've been so strangely silent. But now, I will not let You go until You bless me.

(He pauses at a page, stares at it intently and begins to read. After a moment he pauses, marking the place with a finger, looks up thoughtfully and smiles.

Light down. Music transitions to a church CONGREGATION singing "It Is Well With My Soul.")

CONGREGATION *(singing)*.
>WHEN PEACE, LIKE A RIVER, ATTENDETH MY WAY,
>WHEN SORROWS LIKE SEA BILLOWS ROLL;
>WHATEVER MY LOT, THOU HAS TAUGHT ME TO SAY,
>IT IS WELL, IT IS WELL, WITH MY SOUL.
>IT IS WELL, WITH MY SOUL,
>IT IS WELL, WITH MY SOUL,
>IT IS WELL, IT IS WELL WITH MY SOUL.

(Music out. Light up on the CONGREGATION, a pulpit. FATHER TIM, wearing a robe, enters and crosses to the

Act II   WELCOME TO MITFORD   89

pulpit. He looks out over the CONGREGATION, who wait expectantly.)

FATHER TIM. In the name of the Father, and of the Son, and of the Holy Spirit, amen. *(Crosses himself.)* I have been laboring over a sermon as Jacob wrestled with the angel, but the message would not come together. And the reason it did not is simple: <u>I was writing the wrong sermon.</u> Then at the final hour, when hope was dim and my heart bruised with the sense of failure, God blessed me with a completely different message. He gave me only four words. Here they are, and I pray you will inscribe them on your heart: "In everything…give thanks." And one of those words is the key: *Everything*! Give thanks in everything—in loss of all kinds. In illness, in depression, in grief, in failure. And, of course, in health and peace, success and happiness. Give thanks in everything…*on faith alone*. I want to tell you that I started thanking Him at two o'clock this morning, for something that grieves me deeply. I'm going to continue thanking Him and looking for the good in it. I pray you'll be called to do the same in your lives. Let us say, "Father, I don't know why You're causing, or allowing, this hard thing to happen, but I'm going to give thanks in it because You ask me to. Bottom line, You're God—and that's good enough for me."

(Stage dark. Music up, instrumental version of "It Is Well With My Soul."

Music out, light up on FATHER TIM and CYNTHIA sitting on their bench, holding hands.)

CYNTHIA. Can you believe it...a sophomore.

(Light up on OLDER DOOLEY packing a duffel bag. He wears a college T-shirt.)

FATHER TIM. I remember the day he showed up with his grandfather—barefoot in dirty overalls. Like some special-delivery package that must be opened quickly and handled carefully, lest it perish.

CYNTHIA. Some say you saved Dooley's life.

FATHER TIM. It's more like he saved mine. At the age of sixty, I went from an inward-looking bachelor to an outward-striving father. And then...you moved in next door. A double miracle if there ever was one.

CYNTHIA. I like the result.

FATHER TIM. Yes. *(Beat.)* I re-read Miss Sadie's letter this morning...about the money. She said, "I am depending on you never to mention this to him until he is old enough to bear it with dignity."

CYNTHIA. And?

FATHER TIM. I think it's time.

CYNTHIA. I think you're right.

(She kisses him. Light down on CYNTHIA as FATHER TIM crosses to DOOLEY, who zips up his duffel bag.)

FATHER TIM. Ready, son?

DOOLEY. Just about. Guess I need to hit the road.

FATHER TIM. Got your shaving kit?

DOOLEY *(grinning)*. Yes sir.

FATHER TIM. Last two times, we had to overnight it to you. Money?

DOOLEY *(patting his pocket).* Hundred from you, hundred from Cynthia. Thanks again. And Puny made me a chocolate cake. It'll be history by the time I reach campus.

FATHER TIM. Sit for a moment before you go. *(They sit. FATHER TIM stares at his hands pensively.)*

DOOLEY *(quizzical look).* Dad, are you okay?

FATHER TIM *(smiling).* Giving thanks for everything. And...anticipating.

DOOLEY. Anticipating what?

FATHER TIM. My marching orders. Bishop Cullen says he has something for me, but he hasn't said exactly what.

DOOLEY. He will. People really need what you have to give.

FATHER TIM. Which is what?

DOOLEY. God. You give people God.

FATHER TIM. Thanks, son, for your encouragement...and for coming into my life and changing it utterly.

DOOLEY. I love you, Dad.

FATHER TIM. Love you back. *(DOOLEY glances at his watch and starts to rise. FATHER TIM stops him with a hand on his arm.)* Just one other thing, Dooley. Have you enjoyed your summer working with Hal Owen?

DOOLEY. He's a genius. I've learned so much.

FATHER TIM. Hal tells me he's retiring in five years. That's a year short of when you get your degree. How would you like to have his practice?

DOOLEY. It would be a dream. It's perfect, everything I could ever want. But...

FATHER TIM. What if you had the money to buy it? *(A puzzled look from DOOLEY.)* Let me tell you about a dream Miss Sadie had. It was her dream to see one

Dooley Barlowe be all he can be, to be all God made him to be. She believed in you. *(Beat.)* She left you what will soon be two million dollars. *(A long silence. DOOLEY is stunned, speechless.)* What do you think?

DOOLEY. There's no *way* I can think. You aren't kidding me, are you?

FATHER TIM. I wouldn't kid about these numbers.

DOOLEY. I was just a scrawny little kid who cleaned out her attic and hauled her ashes. Why would she do it?

FATHER TIM. I can't make it any simpler. She believed in you. She believed you would make your way in the world, and she wanted you to have resources.

DOOLEY. Man!

FATHER TIM. You want to go out in the yard and holler…or something?

DOOLEY. I feel…like I want to bust out crying.

FATHER TIM. You can do that. I'll cry with you.

(They embrace. Light down on them, up on CYNTHIA on the bench. FATHER TIM crosses to her and sits pondering for a moment, staring at the floor, while she watches. Then he straightens.)

FATHER TIM *(cont'd)*. Stuart called. He has a job for me.

(CYNTHIA waits, finally punching him playfully on the shoulder)

CYNTHIA. And? And?
FATHER TIM. He wants me to be a vicar.
CYNTHIA. And what, pray tell, is a vicar?

FATHER TIM. The priest of a church that isn't a parish church. A clergyman in charge of a chapel.

CYNTHIA. A particular chapel?

FATHER TIM. Yes. In a rural area near Mitford. The chapel is called Holy Trinity.

(Music up. Light down on the bench, up on a church door. FATHER TIM and CYNTHIA cross to it, stop and look. Music under.)

FATHER TIM *(cont'd)*. It has stood empty for nearly forty years. The challenge is to fill it with people, and together as a family, fill it with the Lord.

CYNTHIA. How do you feel about it?

FATHER TIM. Dumbfounded. And scared silly, to tell the plain truth.

CYNTHIA. Remember the passage from the book we read together not long ago: "There are three stages in the work of God: impossible, difficult, done." I have faith in you.

FATHER TIM. I am thankful for you…beyond words.

CYNTHIA. Here we are, two people facing the unknown, holding hands. I find it all too wondrous, Timothy, and I feel the greatest peace about your new calling. God has called you to come up higher.

FATHER TIM. Then let's go in.

(They pass through the doors arm in arm. Light down on them. Music up and out. Curtain down.)

THE END

DIRECTOR'S NOTES

DIRECTOR'S NOTES

DIRECTOR'S NOTES

TASV@aol.com
Terry - President
    FMCP

Joyce   JSullivan@comporium.net
           Committe member for script submission

           ocw.mit.edu
             for drama courses

performances: MARCH 13, 14, 15   7:30
548-8102   20, 21, 22   7:30
                      23   3:00